The Art of Letting Grow

Integration Books

STUDIES IN PASTORAL PSYCHOLOGY,
THEOLOGY, AND SPIRITUALITY

Robert J. Wicks,
General Editor

also in this series

Clinical Handbook of Pastoral Counseling
R. Wicks, R. Parsons, and D. Capps (Eds.)
Adolescents in Turmoil,
Parents Under Stress
by Richard D. Parsons
Pastoral Marital Therapy
by Stephen Treat and Larry Hof
The Art of Clinical Supervision
edited by Barry Estadt, John Compton
and Melvin Blanchette

The Art of Passingover

An Invitation to Living Creatively

Francis Dorff, O. Praem.

Integration Books

paulist press / new york / mahwah

Library of Congress Cataloging-in-Publication Data

Dorff, Francis.
    The art of passingover: an invitation to living creatively/
Francis Dorff.
        p.   cm.—(Integration books)
        ISBN 0-8091-2958-2 (pbk.)
        1. Spiritual life—Catholic authors.   I. Title.   II. Series.
BX2350.2.D646 1988
248.4'82—dc19   87-32898
                                                                       CIP

Published by Paulist Press
997 Macarthur Boulevard
Mahwah, New Jersey 07430

Printed and bound in the
United States of America

Contents

In loving memory of
Joseph E. Dorff, O. Praem.
brother, priest, confrere, mentor, friend,
whose Passingover
still moves me deeply

I am no longer trying for perfection
by my own efforts. . . .
All I want is to know Christ
and the power of his resurrection
and to share his sufferings
by reproducing the pattern of his death.
That is the way I can hope
to take my place
in the resurrection of the dead.

Philippians 3:9–11
(Jerusalem Bible)

Foreword

The Art of Passingover is not a book about a spiritual process; it is a spiritual experience in itself. It is not designed to dissect the process of transformation; it is, instead, an opening to that very process.

Fran Dorff was asked to prepare the first primarily spiritually-oriented book for the series because both the series and he seemed to be ready; the timing appeared to be ideal. After becoming involved in this book, I think you will appreciate why I say this. To be sure, you will see the sound psychology woven through it, but more than a growth-oriented book, the aim is really beyond growth; it seeks a dramatic release in trust by us—or in his words, "Letting go . . . letting be . . . letting grow."

Anthony de Mello in *One Minute Wisdom* (Doubleday, 1985) relates the following dialogue between a disciple and his master:

> "Make a clean break with your past and you will be Enlightened," said the Master.
>
> "I am doing that by degrees."
>
> "Growth is achieved by degrees. Enlightenment is instantaneous."
>
> Later he said, "Take the leap! You cannot cross a chasm in little jumps."[1]

It is this type of leap for enlightenment into the unseen arms of God that Fran Dorff is sharing with us in *The Art of Passingover*.

Father Dorff is well known for his retreats, workshops, lectures, articles and tapes. What sets him apart is a special nurtured God-given talent for imagination and story-telling. Whether the story is a product of his creativity or a classic, his telling of it helps those with him to open their hearts to risk letting go so they may live creatively. My hope was that if given the opportunity to write a book, he could do this for more of us who wish to share in his presence so we might better encounter the Presence. I feel he has succeeded in this quite admirably.

Robert J. Wicks
Series Editor

Introduction:
The Experience of Change
and the Art of Passingover

All that matters is that one is created anew.
Galatians 6:15
(New American Bible)

If there is one thing we can safely say about the times in which we live, it is that they are times of great change. The changes we are living through are so rapid, so momentous, and so inevitable that to change or not to change is hardly the question for us anymore. The real question we face these days is how to change in such a way that the personal and spiritual quality of our lives, and of the world in which we live, is enhanced, rather than destroyed, by the changes we are going through. This book on the Art of Passingover is an attempt to face the critically important question of how creative change can take place in our lives.

"Passingover" is a word which has many overtones. For some of us, it recalls the biblical experience of being snatched from bondage and death by God (Exodus 12:23–27). For some of us, it carries the feeling tone of the whole Exodus experience of the Jewish People, and of their celebration of their deliverance in the festival of Passover. For some of us, it suggests the life-giving death of Jesus and Easter joy. For some of us, it is alive with the memory of highly personal "passovers," or transitions, which we have experienced in our own lives, while, for others, it evokes the experience of dying. "Passingover" is a word of many overtones.

The many overtones of "Passingover" reflect how personally and spiritually rich this word actually is. It is a word—and an experience—which has many levels of meaning. In this book, we will build on the many meanings and overtones of Passingover to present it as the Art by which our lives, and the life of the world in which we live, can be creatively transformed.

I now realize that this book is rooted in an experience of Passingover which my brother Joe and I shared fifteen years ago. I was a theologian who was getting tired of the college classroom and planning a sabbatical year; he was an experimental psychologist who was getting tired of working with monkeys and recovering from a heart attack. We were both priests in transition. We spent a good deal of time together during those days, talking of life, puzzling through our confusion, and building the hope that, at some later date, we would work together on developing a spirituality of ordinary, personal experience. Then Joe died. He was fifty-four years old. In memory of him, I decided to pursue the project we had talked about.

Shortly after that, I began being asked to serve as a spiritual director for persons who were going through major life transitions themselves, and to give retreats to help Christians celebrate the mystery of the Passover during Holy Week. Before long, these two ministries began to converge with all the Passovers I had ever known. It was during these prayerful experiences of transition, celebration and convergence that this book originally began to take shape.

The conviction which comes to me out of these experiences is that Passingover is actually a creative art which is meant for everyone. I do not believe that Passingover is for Jews only; nor do I believe that it is for Christians only. I believe that Passingover is for everyone. In fact, I believe that, whenever persons are living creatively, they are practicing the Art of Passingover, whether they know it or not.

As a reflection on the Art of Passingover, this book is actually a confession of how I live and believe. To put it succinctly:

I believe that everyone is called to live creatively;
I believe that living creatively requires that we practice
   the Art of Passingover;
I believe that the Art of Passingover involves:
   "Letting-go" in trust,
   "Letting-be" in hope,
   "Letting-grow" in love;
I believe that, in practicing the Art of Passingover,

we are animated by, and commune with, Life Itself;
I believe that, by practicing the Art of Passingover,
our lives are renewed, our world is re-created,
and the Messiah comes.

This, in a nutshell, is the "little creed" which underlies this book. I do not experience it as something to be proven or defended; I experience it as a conviction to be lived and shared. To me, it reflects a lifeline which knits the Jewish and Christian Peoples together more deeply than many of them seem to realize. More broadly still, it reflects a lifeline which, in one way or another, animates the lives of all the courageous and creative persons and communities I have ever known. I realize that the history, the circumstances, the character, the culture, and the religious beliefs of these diverse persons and Peoples differ tremendously. Underneath all of these very real differences, however, I still experience the common lifeline of Passingover uniting the lives of creative persons in a most remarkable way.

As a confession of faith, these reflections on the Art of Passingover are a personal invitation to live creatively in a time of change. In Part One, we will consider the Eighth Day of Creation as the broadest context in which to appreciate the Art of Passingover. In Part Two, we will describe in greater detail what is involved in the threefold movement of "letting-go" in trust, "letting-be" in hope, and "letting-grow" in love. In Part Three, we will reflect on how we begin to personify the Art of Passingover by growing messianically toward Life, Peace, Freedom, Love, God, and a New Creation.

At the outset, I want to thank Abbot John E. Neitzel, O. Praem., for the time and the permission to do this writing; Robert Wicks, for his support and encouragement; Garry Bolger, Thelma Steiger, Thérèsa Gagnon, and Sister Dolores Burkhardt, S.S.J., for their suggestions on reading the manuscript; Larry Leopold, for drawing the logograph of the Art of Passingover which I was only able to envision; and Bill and Kathy Lidle for the gift of a computer which actually seemed to enjoy doing the many revisions of the text.

Our Lady of Daylesford Abbey
Passion Sunday, 1987

Part I

THE EIGHTH DAY OF CREATION

On Listening and Hearing Creatively

Introduction

There is an ancient Christian tradition which holds that it took eight full days to create the world. It is as though God did not finish the creative work He started in the seven days described in the Book of Genesis. After creating man and woman, God used the seventh day to take a well-earned rest.

While God was resting, men and women went to work in the world. As they worked, the whole world began to fall apart in their hands. It began to change from the cosmos, the ordered universe which God had created, into chaos again. This chaos was different, however. It was no longer the original chaos with which God had worked on the first great days of creation. Now it was *human* chaos. Working creatively with such chaos would require a whole new day. On that day, God would no longer work alone. On that day, God would work through and with human persons to create a whole new world from human chaos. Then a new day would dawn: the Eighth Day of Creation.

There is a haunting refrain which knits together the biblical story of creation: "Evening passed and morning came. . . ." This refrain marks off each of the days of creation. The creative words which usher in the first six days of creation are well known. The question is: What is the creative word which ushers in the Eighth Day of Creation? How does the Eighth Day dawn?

Until we experience the darkness of the seventh day of creation, it is hard for us to notice how the Eighth Day dawns. Until we experience how radically flawed, how chaotic, how unfinished our own lives and the life of the world around us are, we have no need to listen for a creative word. When we experience the chaos and the darkness ourselves, however, we long to hear a creative word; we begin listening to all of life for a word which only our hearts can hear. By listening in this way, we can begin to hear, however faintly, the messianic heartbeat which animates all of creation. It is that heartbeat, above all, which carries the creative word of the Eighth Day. The messianic heartbeat is the first sound of the dawn. When we learn to

9

hear it and welcome it, it is as though the daystar begins to rise in our hearts, and a New Day begins to dawn on us. Evening passes and morning comes—the Eighth Day of Creation.

In order to get a better sense of the experience we are describing here and of what our own role in the Eighth Day of Creation might be, let us consider the two key experiences of creative listening through which the New Day dawns: listening to all of life, and hearing the messianic heartbeat.

Chapter 1

Listening to All of Life

A little boy once approached his Rabbi and asked, "Rabbi, why does God no longer speak to His People? He spoke so beautifully to Abraham. He spoke with such power to Moses. He spoke so clearly to Jeremiah and the prophets. Rabbi, why does God no longer speak to His People?"

The Rabbi shook his head as though he were in pain. "My son," he replied, "it is not that God no longer speaks to His People. It is that no one these days can stoop down low enough to listen. No one . . . can stoop down low enough . . . to listen."

The Silence of God

Whether we approach someone else about it or not, there are times in our lives when many of us share this little boy's question. At such times, God no longer speaks to us as He used to. He may once have spoken beautifully to us in our prayers, but we find that He no longer speaks to us there. He may once have spoken to us with great power through the Bible, but we find that He no longer speaks to us there. He may once have spoken to us clearly through the traditions, the feast days, the life, and the symbols of a believing community, but we find that He no longer speaks to us there.

Times such as these make us feel as though Life Itself has lost its voice. They make us feel like strangers, frightened and engulfed by the silence of God. At such times, we share not only the question, but also the pathos, of the little boy when he asks, "Rabbi, why does God no longer speak to His People?"

If we are to believe the Rabbi's teaching in this little story, then to experience the silence of God is to receive an invitation to stoop down lower than we have ever stooped before. It is to receive an invitation to put our ear, not merely to the ground, but to the ground of our being, and to listen for all we are worth. It is to receive an invitation to listen with all our heart for what only our hearts can hear.

As painful as the experience of the silence of God is at first, it can teach us to listen as we may never have listened before. The silence of God can teach us to listen intently, not just to the Bible, or to the teachings of a believing community, or to those of like mind, but to life, and to all of life. If we let it, the silence of God can teach us to stoop down low enough to learn that God speaks wherever, whenever, however and to whomever God pleases.

Some of us believe that God speaks to us through the Bible, through our worship, through our community, and through our faith. As we experience the silence of God in these areas, however, we begin to wonder whether God can speak anyplace else. Can God speak to us in the marketplace; through the newspapers; through our work; through our enemies; through our doubt, our despair, our hatred; through Atheists and "non believers"; through the rich as well as the poor; through the whites as well as the blacks; through our sorrows, joys, pains, pleasures? Can God speak to us through the ordinary events of our lives? Can God speak through silence?

When we first experience the silence of God, questions like these tend to haunt us. To someone who does not share our sense of loss, these questions may seem to be trivial, but to us they are charged with anguish and anxiety. They are like the questions which haunt the Psalmist throughout the night:

> In times of trouble I pray to the Lord;
> all night long I lift my hands in prayer,
> but I cannot find comfort.
> When I think of God, I sigh;
> when I meditate, I feel discouraged.
>
> He keeps me awake all night;
> I am so worried that I cannot speak.
> I think of days gone by
> and remember years of long ago.

I spend the night in deep thought;
I meditate, and this is what I ask myself:
"Will the Lord always reject us?
Will he never again be pleased with us?
Has he stopped loving us?
Does his promise no longer stand?
Has God forgotten to be merciful?
Has anger taken the place of his compassion?"

Then I said, "What hurts me most is this—
that God is no longer powerful."

Psalm 77:2–10

What also hurts us is that the only reply which we first receive to our soul-searching questions is silence. At times such as these, the choice we have is clear: either we can start making a lot of noise, or we can begin a painstaking journey into the silence.

The Journey into Silence

A young man once approached a Master. "Master," he said, "teach me the way to wisdom."

"If you would like, you may accompany me on my way," the Master replied.

"Oh, thank you, Master!" the disciple exclaimed.

They set out, walking together in silence. Before long, they entered a very dense forest. They walked on and on, without saying a word.

As time went by, the disciple began to lose his patience. "This old man is walking so slowly, we will never get anywhere," he thought to himself. "Besides, he promised to teach me the way to wisdom. It has been days now, and he has not said one word to me! What kind of a teacher is he?"

Just then, the Master stopped. He turned to the disciple and asked, "What do you hear?"

"I do not hear anything in this miserable forest!" the disciple shouted.

The old man nodded. And continued on his way.

They walked on and on, without saying another word. Then, the Master stopped again. "What do you hear now?" he asked.

"I hear the songs of a thousand birds and the wind making music in the trees!" the disciple exclaimed. "This forest is full of life! Thank you, Master. Thank you for bringing me to this beautiful place. Let us stay here."

The old man nodded. And continued on his way.

Together, they walked farther and farther into the forest, without saying a word. Then the Master stopped again. "What do you hear now?" he asked.

"Master, I hear the thunder in the distance. It frightens me to death," the disciple replied.

The old man nodded. And continued on his way.

They walked together, in silence, for a very long time. At length, the Master stopped. "What do you hear now?" he asked.

"I hear the babbling of the brook. It comforts me," the disciple replied.

The old man nodded. And continued on his way.

Together they walked in silence, on and on, deeper and deeper into the forest. Then the Master paused again. "What do you hear now?" he asked.

"I hear the silence at the center of the forest. All is peace," the disciple whispered.

The old man nodded. And continued on his way.

They walked on in the silence together for what may have been many years. Then, one day, the Master stopped. He turned to the disciple and asked, "What do you hear now?"

The disciple turned and smiled gently. He bowed to his Master, without saying a word.

Then the Master bowed to his disciple. "I will no longer have to accompany you on your way," he said.

The disciple nodded. And continued on his way. Alone.

The Eloquence of Silence

If we listen carefully to this story, we find ourselves beginning to marvel at how eloquent the silence of the Master is. It leads this willing, yet bewildered, young disciple through a forest of trees, and expectations, and words, and thoughts, and emotions to the silence at the center of the self. It teaches him to listen, not merely to the awesome sounds of the forest, but also to the innermost stirrings of his heart. It teaches the disciple how to listen, not just to the teachings which he already knows, but to the sounds of life which he ignores.

"The Journey into Silence" is a very short story to tell, but it is a very long story to live. It is a very long journey to move from not listening much at all, to listening attentively to everything that surrounds us. It is a longer journey still to move from listening attentively with our ears, to listening with all our heart. It is a very long journey which we make one step at a time.

When the disciple's response indicates that he has learned to listen with all his heart, the Master recognizes that the silence in which he himself journeys has finally been shared. Then he can go in peace. It is as though the disciple has gradually been led to realize that, at the center of all meaningful speaking, and at the center of all creative listening, is an ineffable silence being shared. How eloquent the silence of the Master is.

Since a story has to end somewhere, most stories like this tend to end just where this little story ended. The real journey into silence, however, seldom ends there; it tends to go on. We can well imagine how clearly, how powerfully, how beautifully, all of life can begin to speak to someone who has learned to listen from the center of a silent self. We can imagine, as well, that as a person as sensitive as this continues on the way, sooner or later someone will approach and say, "Master, teach me the way to wisdom." In all probability, the person will reply, "If you would like, you may accompany me on my way." Then the story of the journey into silence goes on.

Once we have listened to, or lived through, this story of the journey into silence, we often begin to realize how extensive the spiritual tradition actually is which attests to the eloquence of silence. We find it in the Hindu custom of "the silent meeting": at an advanced phase of their work together, the guru and the disciple meet to share nothing but one another's presence and silence. We find it in the Hasidic tradition of "teaching by silence": in *The Chosen*, Chaim Potock describes how a rabbi brings up his very promising son by speaking to him indirectly. We find it in the silence of Jesus, as he refuses to accept any of the customary messianic titles. We find it in many biblical passages which, in one way or another, say, "I have much more to tell you, but you cannot bear it now." We find it in the many "reluctant teacher" stories within the Zen tradition. We find it in the many Taoist variations on the theme, "The one who knows does not speak; the one who speaks does not know." We find it in the tradition of "Grand Silence" in which monks spend most of their lives. Once we have experienced the eloquence of silence, we begin to find it in the most astonishing places.

At first, we begin to wonder whether the silence of God might not be part of this whole ecumenical tradition of teaching by silence. Later on, we begin to suspect that it is the other way around; perhaps this whole ecumenical tradition of teaching by silence is, in fact, part of the silence of God. In that case, the story of the little boy approaching his rabbi might take a somewhat different turn for us:

> The Rabbi shook his head, as though he were in pain. "My son," he said, "it is not that God no longer speaks to His People. It is just that silence is God's favorite language. Now he is letting all of life speak for Him . . . but . . . no one these days can stoop down low enough to listen to all of life. No one . . . can stoop down low enough . . . to listen to the silence."

The Courage To Listen

While, eventually, the experience of silence may be eloquent, at first it is awkward. It puzzles us, bores us, exasperates us, threatens us, frightens us. We experience it not only as an insult to our intelligence but, in some strange way, as a threat to our person. Perhaps this is why it takes so much courage for us to enter into the silence and listen. If we know the comic "The Wizard of Id," we might find ourselves empathizing with the little king in this sequence of cartoons:

> In the middle of the night, a dog barks outside the castle of the little king.
> The king calls down to the guard outside. "Guard, get rid of that dog!"
> "But, Sire," the guard replies, "the dog is protecting you."
> "What is it protecting me from?" the king asks.
> "From the silence, Sire," the guard replies.
> The dog continues barking outside the castle—undisturbed.

Although we may chuckle at this comic strip, many of us share the little king's fear of silence. When we become silent, we have no way of knowing what we will hear—or whether we will hear anything at all. To become silent, we have to stoop down very low; we have to let go of all that we are accustomed to hear. We have to empty ourselves of the customary sounds which tell us who and where we are. We have to risk facing the unknown, hearing the unheard of, and experiencing nothing at all. That prospect is extremely frightening to most of us. At first, it is like entering a vacuum; and nature abhors a vacuum. It is much safer to stay with what we already know, and to listen to what we are accustomed to hear. It is much safer to fill our lives with customary sounds to protect us from listening to the silence at the center, and to whatever else we may be led to hear from there. It is much easier to go about building a sort of sound barrier to protect us from the silence: pet phrases, constant chatter, incessant activity, unending entertainment, background music, and the like, which keep us and others from realizing that we are afraid to listen. In building our own sound barrier, we help create an increasingly noisy world of meaningless sounds to which there is no need to listen. In such a world, we begin to go deaf, and the ability to listen to the unfamiliar and subtler sounds of life becomes a lost art.

We have to have courage to enter into the silence and listen. It is that kind of courage that the Master in our little story communicates to his disciple simply by walking with him, every step of the way. Regardless of what the disciple discovers at any given time, the Master nods acceptingly. It is as though he has been there before. His presence and his silent nod say that it is all right to be there; then he continues on the way. As he does so, the disciple finds the courage to take his next step into the silence.

Listening with All Our Heart

We have seen the disciple led, step by step, through the many kinds of silence to learn the many levels of listening. The Master's simple question "What do you hear now?" is like a master key by which he unlocks for the disciple successively deeper levels of listening. At first, the disciple is so caught up with his own thoughts that he cannot even hear with his ears. Then he is led to listen with his ears, so that he may hear with his heart as the sounds of the forest frighten, comfort, and quiet him. Finally, he is led to listen with all his heart to what he cannot yet hear, or is incapable of describing.

The experience of listening with all our heart is at the very center of the journey into silence. This is a special kind of listening which is very different from the casual, polite, or half-hearted listening which we usually do. It is a passionate kind of listening in which our lives reach toward what can lend them meaning and purpose. It is how the watchman listens for the first sounds of the dawn. It is how a mother listens to hear the heartbeat of her sick child. It is how the disciple learns to listen to the Master and to all of life. It is a soul-searching, life-seeking, whole-hearted listening which gradually renders us totally present and totally attentive to what IS. This is how we listen, when we listen with all our heart.

Listening from Heart to Heart

When we first hear the story of "The Journey into Silence," our attention tends to focus so much on the listening of the disciple that we overlook the listening of the Master. Yet, if we think about it, every step of the way the Master is listening with all his heart to the disciple. He nods to acknowledge that he too can hear what the disciple is hearing, and continues on his way. In listening in this way, the Master is listening to two lives, to two heartbeats, at the same time. He is listening simultaneously to what is going on in his disciple's heart, and to what is going on in his own. This is yet another level of listening; it is a kind of "stereophonic listening" by which we listen, not only with all our heart, but also from heart to heart.

Listening in Stereo

I once asked a storyteller what he was doing in the sometimes extended silence between the questions from his listeners and his replies.

"I try to feel what is going on in their hearts, and what is going on in mine," he replied. "Then I try to speak to that."

Here was a man who was not afraid of heart-searching silence. In fact, his ability to speak heart to heart, through his stories, was rooted in his ability to listen from heart to heart, in the silence. His mastery of the art of storytelling was rooted in his mastery of the art of listening. He was accustomed to listening and speaking "in living stereo."

We may find ourselves thinking, now, of some masters in the art of listening whom we know personally. These are persons who are able to listen simultaneously, both to several levels of life and to several lives; they are persons who are able to listen to life stereophonically.

For one thing, they can listen simultaneously to what is going on outside and inside of us. It is as though, on one channel, they are attuned to what we say, to the tone of our voice, to our moments of silence, to how we look, to our body language, and to all that our outside reveals. On the other channel, they listen, with equal attentiveness, to our thoughts, to our fears, to our fantasies and dreams, to our hopes, our values and our deepest desires, and to all that our inside reveals. Their gentle questions often invite us to listen to something we may not yet be able to hear, or to confirm something they are hearing for the first time. When they say something like, "It sounds to me that, in spite of all of the tension in your life just now, and your desire for greater clarity, you seem to be at peace, basically, with who you are, with what you are doing," we know that they have been listening to much more than our words. They have been listening to our whole lives. Perhaps we ourselves had been so caught up in listening to only one level of our lives that we had been unable to hear what our whole life was actually sounding like.

In addition to being able to listen to several levels of life at the same time, masters in the art of listening are able to listen to at least two lives at a time. We discover this when, from time to time, they respond to what we say by sharing something from their own experience of life. As what they say begins to resonate in our own hearts, we begin to realize that they have been listening to us "from heart to heart," all along; we begin to realize that they have been listening to us "in stereo."

The experience of being listened to from heart to heart suggests yet another version of the story of the little boy who approaches his Rabbi about the silence of God:

> The Rabbi shook his head, as though he were in pain. "My son," he replied, "it is not that God no longer speaks to His People. It is that He is listening to His People now. And what do His People have to say to Him? What do His People . . . have to say?"

When we are working our way through major changes in our lives, those who listen to us from heart to heart are a very special gift. The way in which they listen to us is not only supportive; it is creative. It evokes from us experiences and insights of which we thought ourselves incapable. It gives us the space and the time to broaden our horizons and to deepen our perspective. It lets us experience the paradox that, at critical moments of growth in our lives, we can be both alone and not alone. It honors the integrity of our lives as they move through painful places. By their example, these dedicated listeners invite us to stoop down very low; they invite us to listen with all our heart to all of life, at a time when we may be listening to only one aspect of our lives, if we are listening to life at all. As we learn from their example, we begin listening to life, as they do: with all our heart and from heart to heart; we begin listening to life in stereo.

In time, we may find that God begins to speak to us again, in the most unlikely places, through the most unlikely persons, in the most unlikely ways. We may find that God begins to speak to us through the ordinary experiences of our everyday lives.

When this happens, we frequently begin to wonder whether what has become a closed book for us may again become a living Word. We begin to wonder whether God can speak to us personally, through the Bible. It then becomes time for us to open the Book again, and to listen to it, heart to heart.

Chapter 2

Hearing the Messianic Heartbeat

The Heartbeat of the Great Rabbi

There once was a little boy named Mordechai. His parents loved him dearly. He was the perfect child, except for one thing. He refused to study the Word of God. It did not matter to him that all the boys his age were studying Torah. He would not do it. His parents promised to give him anything he wanted. They threatened him with everything he didn't want. If only he would study Torah. But, come what may, little Mordechai would not study the Word of God.

The parents were at their wits' end. They did not know what else to do. Then, one day, they heard that the Great Rabbi was going to visit their village. They were delighted. "Surely he will be able to get little Mordechai to read Torah," they said to one another.

When the Great Rabbi arrived, the parents took little Mordechai to him. "Our son is a fine boy," they explained, "except for one thing. He refuses to study the Word of God."

"You give this boy to me," the Rabbi shouted, "and I will teach him a lesson he will never forget!"

The parents were frightened by the Rabbi's rage. "Should we give our little Mordechai to this angry bear of a man?" they asked themselves. "Yet, what else can we do?" So they handed little Mordechai over to the Rabbi.

The Rabbi grabbed the boy, led him into the next room, and slammed the door behind them.

Little Mordechai stood in the corner of the room trembling. The Rabbi just stood there looking at him. Then the Rabbi stretched himself out on the floor.

"Mordechai," he whispered, "come here."

The little boy inched his way over to where the Rabbi lay. The Rabbi opened his arms and said, "Lie down, Mordechai. Lie down."

Without saying a word, Mordechai lay down in the Rabbi's arms. The Rabbi folded his arms around the little boy and held him silently, against his heart.

After a while, the Rabbi stood up. He took little Mordechai by the hand and led him to the door. Then, all of a sudden, he flung open the door and threw the little boy into the room where his parents were waiting.

"I have taught this boy a lesson he will never forget!" the Rabbi shouted. "You mark my words. From this day on, he will study Torah!"

And so it was. Little Mordechai studied the Word of God as no one in the village had ever studied it before. He learned it all by heart. His parents were so proud of him. They would point to the text on one page, and little Mordechai would quote what was written on the other side of the page without even looking at it.

As years went by, Mordechai himself became a great Rabbi. People would come from far and wide to bring him their problems, to pose their questions, and to marvel at the depth of his wisdom, as he interpreted the Word of God for them. In their amazement, they would often ask, "Rabbi, who taught you to read Torah?"

Then Mordechai would smile, and say, "I first learned to read Torah, when the Great Rabbi held me . . . silently . . . against his heart. . . . I first learned to read Torah . . . when the Great Rabbi . . . held me . . . silently . . . against his heart."

The Messianic Heartbeat

In this story, little Mordechai is invited to stoop down lower than many of us may be willing to stoop. He stoops down low enough to hear the heartbeat of the Great Rabbi. That heartbeat teaches him that the Torah is not just written in a book; it is written in the hearts of those who live by God's Word. The heartbeat of the Great Rabbi gives little Mordechai the desire and the energy to change; it gives him what all the promises and all the threats of his well-intentioned parents were unable to give. It teaches him to take the Word of God to heart by reading it from the inside out.

After hearing this little story, we can hardly help wondering: What would we hear if we could listen to the heartbeat of the Great Rabbi? What would we hear if we could listen to the heartbeat of those who live by God's Word—to the heartbeat of Abraham, or Moses, or Israel, or David, or the Psalmist, or Jeremiah, or the Baptizer, or Jesus, or his disciples? What would we hear if we could listen with all our heart, not merely to the words of the Bible, but to the heartbeat within the Bible itself, and to the heartbeat of the many communities for which it is a source of life?

If we listen with all our heart to the Bible, underneath all of its words, we can hear the messianic heartbeat. It is the heartbeat of Passingover; it sounds like this: l-e-t-t-i-n-g-g-o . . . l-e-t-t-i-n-g-b-e . . . l-e-t-t-i-n-g-g-r-o-w. It is a whole-hearted human response to the word which ushers in the Eighth Day of Creation: "Let go; Let be; Let grow." This is the word behind all the words in the Bible; it is the story behind all the biblical stories. This is the heartbeat which animates all of scripture. If we listen carefully, we may be able to hear this messianic heartbeat within a few keynote passages of scripture.

The Heartbeat of Abraham

Now the Lord said to Abram,
"Go from your country and your kindred and your
    father's house
        (L-e-t-t-i-n-g-g-o)
to the land that I will show you.
        (L-e-t-t-i-n-g-b-e)
And I will make of you a great nation, and I will bless
    you, and

make your name great, so that you will be a
  blessing. . . . "
    (L-e-t-t-i-n-g-g-r-o-w)
So Abram went, as the Lord had told him. . . .
    (P-a-s-s-i-n-g-o-v-e-r)

Genesis 12:1–2, 4 (R.S.V.)

This is the heartbeat of a truly Great Rabbi. It is the heartbeat
of the father of all who believe in Yahweh's creative power. As we
know, Abraham was childless and his wife Sarah was beyond the age
of childbearing at this time. In light of that, Yahweh's promise was a
most unlikely promise; and Abraham's fidelity was a most creative
fidelity. After so many centuries, this creative fidelity still continues
to animate a People that has become as numerous as the stars.

The Heartbeat of Moses and Israel

As he stands barefoot before the burning bush, Moses hears the
voice of the God of Abraham, the God of Isaac and the God of Jacob
telling him to go to the Pharaoh to bring Yahweh's People out of
Egypt.

Moses doubts his own ability to accomplish this mission
    (L-e-t-t-i-n-g-g-o)
but Yahweh assures him, "I will be with you," and that
    (L-e-t-t-i-n-g-b-e)
he will lead the people to worship God on this very mountain.
    (L-e-t-t-i-n-g-g-r-o-w)
Then Moses leads his people from Egypt to covenant with
  God.
    (P-a-s-s-i-n-g-o-v-e-r)

See Exodus 3–4; 12–24

This is the heartbeat of another giant of a man. Moses is the man
through whom Yahweh works not only to liberate the people of Israel, but also to establish them as God's Chosen People in a most
intimate way, through the Covenant at Sinai. In the Exodus expe-

rience, the Passingover of Moses becomes the Passingover of a whole nation, its most formative religious experience, its primary example of spiritual growth and fidelity, and its most celebrated festival of how God's creative power unfolds within His People. For Israel, after Moses, Yahweh is not only "the God of our Fathers," but He is, especially, the God of the Exodus Experience, the God of the Covenant, and the God of Passingover. In the Exodus Experience, Passingover becomes the heartbeat of Israel.

The Heartbeat of David

In Psalm fifty one, the Psalmist lets us listen to King David as he sings his heart out after sinning with Bathsheba:

> Be merciful to me, O God, because of your constant love.
> Because of your great mercy wipe away my sins!
> Wash away all my evil
> and make me clean from my sin!. . . .
>   (L-e-t-t-i-n-g-g-o)
> Create a pure heart in me, O God,
> and put a new and loyal spirit in me. . . .
>   (L-e-t-t-i-n-g-b-e)
> Give me again the joy that comes from your salvation,
> and make me willing to obey you.
> Then I will teach sinners your commands,
> and they will turn back to you.
>   (L-e-t-t-i-n-g-g-r-o-w)
> Spare my life, O God, and save me,
> and I will gladly proclaim your righteousness.
> Help me to speak, Lord,
> and I will praise you.
>   (P-a-s-s-i-n-g-o-v-e-r)

In this passage we can hear the heartbeat of the King at a turning point in his life. The turning point is one of repentance in which David moves from letting go of his infidelity, through letting God's creative and healing power be within him, to letting a life of recon-

ciling service grow. This is a movement of repentance, an experience
of Passingover which is animated by the messianic heartbeat.

The Heartbeat of Jeremiah

At a critical point in his ministry as a prophet, Jeremiah's heartbeat sounds like this:

Lord, you have deceived me, and I was deceived. You are
stronger than I am, and you have overpowered me.
(L-e-t-t-i-n-g-g-o)
Everyone makes fun of me; they laugh at me all day long.
Whenever I speak, I have to cry out and shout, "Violence!
Destruction!" Lord, I am ridiculed and scorned all the time
because I proclaim your message. But when I say, "I will
forget the Lord and no longer speak in his name," then
your message is like a fire burning deep within me. I try
my best to hold it in, but can no longer keep it back.
(L-e-t-t-i-n-g-b-e)
. . . But you, Lord, are on my side, strong and mighty, and
those who persecute me will fail. . . . Sing to the Lord!
Praise the Lord!
(L-e-t-t-i-n-g-g-r-o-w)
Jeremiah 20:7–9, 11, 13

These words show the prophet moving through very troubled
waters. In his own life, he seems to be going through the pain which
his whole People will experience shortly, as the enemy invades Jerusalem, destroys the Temple, and takes them North into captivity.
Then Jeremiah's personal Passingover becomes a prophetic pathway
through troubled waters for his people, as he prophesies the return
home from exile, the rebuilding of Jerusalem, and a New Covenant
which will be written on the people's hearts. During these troubled,
yet most creative, times, we can hear the messianic heartbeat ani-

mating the life of Jeremiah. This heartbeat enables him to animate
the "dry bone" of his people in exile, and the lives of a host of spiritual pilgrims ever since.

The Heartbeat of the Baptizer

People's hopes began to rise, and they began to wonder
whether John perhaps might be the Messiah. So John said
to all of them, "I baptize you with water, but someone is
coming who is much greater than I am.
 (L-e-t-t-i-n-g-g-o)
I am not good enough even to untie his sandals.
 (L-e-t-t-i-n-g-b-e)
He will baptize you with the Holy Spirit and fire."
 (L-e-t-t-i-n-g-g-r-o-w)

Luke 3:15–17

At a much later date, John's sense of his own mission and identity is put even more succinctly:

"He must become more
 important
while I become less important."
 (P-a-s-s-i-n-g-o-v-e-r)
 John 3:30

The Heartbeat of Jesus

At a critical time in his ministry, Jesus begins to make the following prophecy:

"The Son of Man
will be handed over to men
 (L-e-t-t-i-n-g-g-o)
who will kill him.
 (L-e-t-t-i-n-g-b-e)

Three days later, however, he will rise to life."
  (L-e-t-t-i-n-g-g-r-o-w)
But they did not understand what this teaching meant,
and they were afraid to ask him.

Mark 9:31–33

From this point on, the Gospels portray the life of Jesus as a "baptism by fire": a progressive Passingover by which he embodies for his well-meaning disciples the heartbeat they could not yet hear. When they finally are able to hear the heartbeat of Jesus again, the disciples make his Passingover the primary object of their preaching (Acts 3:12–26; 4:8–12; 5:29–32; 10:34–43; 13:16–41).

The Messianic Life Cycle

In time, the belief of those who consider Jesus to be the Messiah grows in two directions. It reaches backward, to before the beginning of time, and forward, to the end of all time. In this way, the messianic life cycle is believed to embrace all of time, and the messianic heartbeat is believed to animate all of creation. We can hear the full messianic life cycle beginning to resonate in this early baptismal hymn:

Have this mind among yourselves,
which is yours in Christ Jesus
who, though he was in the form of God,
did not count equality with God
a thing to be grasped.
  (L-e-t-t-i-n-g-g-o)
but emptied himself,
taking the form of a servant,
being born in the likeness of men.
  (L-e-t-t-i-n-g-g-o)
And being found in human form
he humbled himself
and became obedient unto death,
even death on a cross.

(L-e-t-t-i-n-g-g-o . . .
    L-e-t-t-i-n-g-b-e)
Therefore God has highly exalted him
and bestowed on him the name
above every name,
        (L-e-t-t-i-n-g-g-r-o-w)
that at the name of Jesus
every knee should bow,
in heaven and on earth
and under the earth,
        (L-e-t-t-i-n-g-g-r-o-w)
and every tongue confess
that Jesus Christ is Lord,
to the glory of God the Father.
        (P-a-s-s-i-n-g-o-v-e-r)
                Philippians 2:5–11 (R.S.V.)

We can see how this hymn begins to reflect the full messianic
life cycle. First, there is a cosmic "stooping low": a complete down-
ward movement of humiliation through the Messiah's voluntary self-
emptying by being born and by dying on the cross. Then, the cycle
completes itself in an upward movement of exaltation by God's raising the Messiah from the dead to reign as the Lord of all creation.
The early Christian community believes that it is by moving through
this cycle that God's creative Word becomes incarnate in Jesus; that
Jesus becomes the Messiah; and that the Messiah becomes the Lord
of all creation. It is through this messianic life cycle that evening
passes and morning comes, inaugurating the Eighth Day of Creation.

We can simplify this portrait of the messianic life cycle by vis-
ualizing it like this:

If this approach to the experience of Passingover makes one thing clear, it is that Passingover is not just a doctrine, a dogma, or an occasional feast day. It is a personal and a communal life cycle which is to be taken to heart.

When we hear the messianic heartbeat as it resonates throughout the Bible, we begin to realize that it is a fully human response to the word which ushers in the Eighth Day of Creation: "Let go; Let be; Let grow." This is the word at the center of the experience of Passingover. It is the word by which God re-creates the world from human chaos. The way in which the world is re-created, however, is through persons who listen to this word with all their heart, and give it a whole-hearted response through their lives. In this way, the messianic heartbeat becomes their own and they become artists in the Art of Passingover.

The Stereo Effect

A hiker was once walking in the hills, when he came upon a man who had strung a rope across a very deep chasm.

"You are not going to try to cross that chasm on that little rope, are you?" the hiker asked.

"Of course I am," the man replied. He balanced himself on the rope and carefully inched his way to the other side and back again.

"That was marvelous! Absolutely marvelous! You are an artist!" the hiker exclaimed.

The other man smiled, and began to fill a wheelbarrow with big rocks.

"What are you going to do now?" the hiker asked.

"I am going to go across with the wheelbarrow," he replied.

The hiker held his breath as the man moved the rock-filled wheelbarrow onto the rope and gradually began making his way to the other side.

"One false move now, and he is a goner," the hiker thought to himself.

But the man made it to the other side and back, without even a pause.

"I have never seen anything like that in my life!" the hiker exclaimed. "What courage! You are, without a doubt, the greatest tightrope walker in the world!"

"Do you really think so?" the man asked.

"Of course I do," the hiker replied. "You have perfect balance. You are fantastic!"

"Do you believe that I could take you across to the other side in my wheelbarrow?" the tightrope walker asked.

"I certainly do," the hiker answered. "If you can make it across with those rocks, you can certainly make it across with me. They are much heavier than I am."

"Good," the tightrope walker said, turning the wheelbarrow around. "Then, get in."

We do not have to be told that *that* is a different story. It is one thing for us to believe, in principle, that the tightrope walker can take us across to the other side; it is something else for us to get in the wheelbarrow and let it happen.

When we get attached to the Bible, it is relatively easy for us to get caught up in admiring and celebrating the courage and creativity of Abraham, Moses, Israel, David, Jeremiah, the Baptizer, Jesus, the early Christians, and a host of others. In this way, it is relatively easy for us to miss the whole point of the biblical story of Passingover. The whole point of that story is that these giants of creative fidelity are all members of one Passingover family, and that we are next in line; the whole point of the story is to invite us to "get in." In the Gospel of John, Jesus makes this point for his disciples in a very graphic way. As he prepares with them for his own Passingover, he stoops down to wash their feet. Then he gets up and joins them again at table. With that, he says to them.

"Do you know what I have done to you? You call me Teacher and Lord; and you are right, for so I am. If I then, your Lord and Teacher, have washed your feet, you also

ought to wash one another's feet. For I have given you an example, that you also should do as I have done to you."
                                                                John 13:12–15 (R.S.V.)

Within a few hours, he would begin giving them an even more exacting example to follow by stooping down still lower. This is his way of saying, "Get in."

When we begin to hear the messianic heartbeat that animates the biblical experience of Passingover, therefore, we are receiving an invitation to "get in." If only for a moment, it is as though we begin to hear our lives "in stereo." On the one channel, we hear the personal experiences of Passingover which are at the heart of our own lives; on the other channel, we hear the more-than-personal experiences of Passingover which are at the heart of the biblical tradition. At such times, we begin to feel that the messianic heartbeat and our own are somehow strangely related. It is as though we are no longer reading the Bible; the Bible is reading us. This is part of the "stereo effect" which comes with hearing our life unfolding simultaneously at both a personal and a messianic level. We may realize that this "stereo effect" is only an invitation, and that it requires a response from us to be complete, but even the invitation adds a new depth, a new richness, and a more-than-personal resonance to our life. This is one of the ways in which God begins to speak to his people again.

The Stereo Response

If the "stereo effect" is an invitation to "get in" and to become an active participant in re-creating the world by Passingover, the "stereo response" is a personal decision to accept this invitation. It is a decision to listen to the creative word "Let go; Let be; Let grow" in such a way that we become partners in the messianic work of the Eighth Great Day. This is what it means to believe, when we are experiencing the "stereo effect"; it means giving a stereo response to the word by which God re-creates the world. It means having the courage to live by Passingover.

In these first two chapters, we have been reflecting on the kind of creative listening and hearing which are involved in realizing the Eighth Day of Creation. In the next three chapters, we will describe, in greater detail, the courage it takes for us to listen and hear in this way, so that we may live creatively by Passingover.

Part II

THE ART OF PASSINGOVER

*On "Letting-go"; "Letting-be";
and "Letting-grow"*

Introduction

When it comes to being an artist, it is not simply enough for us to get the general idea of the art. Art is beauty in action, so to become an artist, we have to get into the action and become very attentive to the quality of the individual actions which make up the art. We usually do that by imitating someone, and by repeating the whole series of actions which they model for us. In time, we become more graceful in our actions, and lose our original awkwardness. The art becomes quite natural to us.

The same is true of the Art of Passingover: to know what this art is actually all about, it is simply not enough "to get the general idea." We have to get into the action, and become especially attentive to the quality of each of the actions involved in the Art of Passingover. The traditional way of doing this is to observe a Master in action and to imitate the actions of the Master until they become second nature to us. Then the Art of Passingover becomes our own, and the many different actions involved in it become a unified whole for us.

We have seen that, from a biblical point of view, the Art of Passingover involves a three-fold action of "Letting-go," "Letting-be," and "Letting-grow," coordinated into one graceful movement: the movement by which God re-creates the world. In this section, we want to listen to the distinct quality of each of these three actions to see whether we can pick up a "stereo effect" between our own experience of life and the messianic experience of Passingover. We will first consider "Letting-Go: The Experience of Painful Endings," then, "Letting-Be: The Experience of Awkward Inbetweens," and, finally, "Letting-Grow: The Experience of Awesome Beginnings."

In general, our approach will be the same in each chapter. First of all, we will listen to our personal experience of life on "Channel One." Then, we will listen to the more-than-personal, messianic experience of life on "Channel Two." Finally, we will suggest what the "stereo response" of believing involves at that particular point in our lives. Perhaps, along the way, we will discover that, without even knowing it, we have been practicing the Art of Passingover all along.

Chapter 3

Letting-Go
The Experience of Painful Endings

> I look to the mountains;
> where will my help come from?
> My help will come from the Lord,
> who made heaven and earth.
>
> *Psalm 121:1–2*

One day, an experienced mountain climber was climbing a mountain. He was quite proud of himself. He had not been climbing all that long, yet he was already halfway to the top.

Just then, he lost his footing and began to fall. As he fell, he reached out and grabbed onto the branch of a tree. There he hung, halfway between heaven and earth. He was unable to climb up. He was unable to climb down. All that he could do was to hang on for dear life.

After a while, he looked down into the valley below and called out, "Help! Is there anybody down there who can help me? Is there *anybody* down there who can help me?"

He listened intently, but all he could hear was the sound of his own frightened voice echoing through the valley, " . . . who can help me? . . . who can help me?" Then, nothing but silence, and the sound of the wind.

So he looked up toward the top of the mountain. "Help!" he cried, "Is there anybody up there who can help me? Is there *anybody* up there?"

From the top of the mountain, a voice said, "I am here. Do not be afraid."

"Who are you?" the climber asked.

"I am the Lord," the voice replied.

"Wonderful!" the climber exclaimed. "Listen, Lord, I'm in trouble, here. Can you help me?"

"Of course I can help you," the voice answered. "Just do as I say."

"I'll do anything you say, if only you will help me," the climber replied.

Then the voice said, "Let go."

For a long while, the climber was silent. Then he called back, "Is there anybody *else* up there who can help me?"

On Climbing Mountains

As we hear this story, we may chuckle to ourselves; we may hear the sound of our own voice in the mountain climber's reply. It may be that he has the courage to say what we often think when we begin to hear the word "let go" in our own lives: "Forget it!"

This little story is much more than a punch line, however; it is a story of a very long journey and of an invitation to make a journey of a very different kind.

The long journey which is involved in this story is a journey of personal achievement. The mountain climber is a person who has clearly taken hold of his own life. He is "in command." He is an experienced climber who is justifiably proud of his accomplishments. He is already halfway to the top of the mountain! Then he hits a problem which makes it clear that he will not be able to get to the top of this mountain on his own. He finds himself crying out for help. This cry for help is a turning point in the life of someone who has become accustomed to being the master of his own fate. The cry for help is followed by a promise of help. With the promise comes an immediate sense of relief. The relief is short-lived, however, since the promise is followed by a paradox: help will come only if the mountain climber is willing to "let go" of his own grip on things. This paradox of progress through "letting-go" is an invitation to a whole new type of journey. The mountain climber seems to recognize that; in effect, his response is, "Forget it!" That is the punch line. Apart from the long journey of personal achievement which precedes it, however, this punch line would not have much punch at all.

The storyline we have been describing is basically one of achievement-problem-promise-paradox. If we are to experience the full impact of the word "let go," it is very important to remember this underlying flow of events. Apart from this storyline, the word "let go" strikes us as either a sick joke or a pious nosegay. As part of this storyline, however, "let go" is a challenge to a whole new way of living.

First of all, it is important that we remember the background of personal achievement in this story. Had the mountain climber not already made a long journey toward taking hold of his own life, he would have had little or nothing to "let go" of. Had he not built his muscles to see how high he could climb "on his own," he would have had no way of knowing when he had reached his own limits and was in need of help.

It is important that we remember the problem, too. Had the mountain climber not come across a situation which he could not handle on his own, the story simply would have been one of "climbing as usual." As it is, the problem of reaching his own limits threatens the mountain climber's well-established storyline of personal achievement and calls for a very different approach. The experience of a problem which requires more-than-personal resources marks a turning point in the journey of personal achievement.

It is important that we remember the promise as well. It is the promise, above all, that lets the mountain climber hear the word "let go." Apart from the promise, "let go" is an arbitrary invitation to suicide. Only a fool would listen to it. Against the background of the promise, however, "let go" becomes a paradoxical invitation to a very different kind of journey.

Finally, it is important that we remember the paradox itself. That is what the word "let go" becomes when we are in touch with the whole storyline of achievement-problem-promise: a paradox.

Against the background of achievement-problem-promise-paradox, we can see that the mountain climber is being asked to "let go" of much more than the branch of a tree. He is being asked to "let go" of his whole approach to life.

1. Channel One: The Personal Experience of "Letting-Go"

I was struck by one of my nieces' reaction to the story of the mountain climber. "Right on!" she said. "I'll be damned if I'll let go!"

My niece had gotten the point. She had listened to this story from within her own experience of life and had recognized it to be much more than an "amusing little story." She recognized it to be a threat to all she had worked so hard to accomplish. Hers was an honest and spontaneous reaction to the very powerful and demanding first word of the Eighth Day of Creation: "Let go."

When she first heard this story, my niece was still quite young, and was working very hard at building a life of her own. It could be that she had not yet taken hold of her own life, and was in no position to listen to "let go." Perhaps she had not yet come face to face with her own limits or had already heard too many people tell her too early, too often, and too glibly to "let go." It is hard to say. At any rate, she had gotten the point; she had listened well.

As we listen to the story of the mountain climber from within our own experience of life, we may find ourselves sharing my niece's reaction to it. It is no joke to be asked to "let go" of what we have struggled hard to achieve. It is no joke to be asked to "let go" of things, and habits and persons we have come to love and enjoy. It is no joke to be asked to "let go" of our hard-won control on life. So what, if we seem to be stuck at a certain point in our lives? "It's better to be stuck than sorry," we might say; or, "There must be a better way!"; or, more forcefully still, "I'll be damned if I'll let go!"

There is a certain advantage in hearing the word "let go" in a story like this. We can always say, "It is *just* a story." Then we can try to forget it and go about our everyday lives, climbing or clinging in the hope of never having to hear "let go" again.

The "let go" we are talking about, however, is not a word that comes, once in a lifetime, from a storybook God on top of a mythical mountain; it is a word that comes again and again, from the center of our own life. This is what we mean when we speak of hearing the word "let go" on Channel One; we mean hearing it coming from the middle of our own life story. As a rule, this "let go" is not a laughing matter, and is much more difficult to evade.

"Letting-Go" on Many Levels

Just as there are many levels on which we can listen to life, so there are many levels on which we can hear "let go" resonating within our own life. At times we may hear life asking us to "let go" with our hands, that is, to "let go" of that to which we have become *physically* attached. At other times we may hear life asking us to "let go" with our heads, that is, to "let go" of that to which we have become *mentally* attached. At still other times we may hear life asking us to "let go" with our hearts, that is, to "let go" of that to which we have become *emotionally* attached. At still other times we may hear life asking us to "let go" with all of our being. At such times we are being asked to "let go" *spiritually* of whole phases of our life—perhaps of our whole way of life, or, even, of our life as a whole.

"Letting-Go" Physically

Perhaps the loudest invitation to "let go" comes from our bodies. For some reason or other, it is also one of the hardest invitations for most of us to hear. Maybe we are just too close to our bodies to hear what they have to say, or maybe we have never thought of our bodies as having anything worthwhile to say in the first place. At any rate, it seems that many of us find it hard to hear the language of our body, especially when it is telling us to "let go."

To take an example, our body ages. As it ages, we find that we are no longer able to look or act the way we did before. This is our body's way of inviting us to "let go" of what we once were. Since a good deal of our identity is rooted in our physical appearance and prowess, most of us do not appreciate this invitation to "let go." The fact that we live in a culture which idealizes youth makes us even less inclined to accept this invitation. We often respond to it by exploring all kinds of ways to hold onto the looks and the energies of earlier years. At first, some of our heroic efforts to resist "letting-go" physically may seem quite admirable. As we prolong them, however, they tend to become increasingly pathetic. It is one thing to be "the belle of the ball" at nineteen; it is something else to be acting that way at fifty. It is one thing to be a promising athlete in high school; it is something else to pretend that thirty years have not made a difference.

At first, these comments about "letting-go" physically may make us think of celebrated athletes, dancers, and singers who did not know when to "let go." If we think about it a bit, however, most of us will find that what is written large in the lives of many "celebrities" is written quite legibly in our own lives as well.

To take another example, our body not only ages, it dies. Furthermore, it reminds us of that fact from time to time, especially when we continue to make unreal demands of it. At such times our body frequently gets sick or breaks down. It is as though it tries to remind us that we are human, and mortal. If we listen closely to our body at such times, we can often hear it inviting us to "let go" of something we are currently doing or clinging to, so that we may be healthy and strong again.

A friend of mine was a classic example of this. As a young man, he was living a very hectic life in some very stressful circumstances when he developed a crippling case of arthritis. The doctors said that they could do nothing for it. They prescribed pain-killers which he was to take for the rest of his life. He was told that the medicine would make him somewhat drowsy most of the time, but that it would lessen his pain. Not content with that solution, the man took a year's leave of absence from his work. During that time, he got some rest, searched his soul, and changed his life style, his diet and his job. He now experiences the arthritic pain only as a warning signal that he is "pushing it" again. Through his experience of sickness, he has learned to listen to his body's invitation to "let go."

We can enlarge a bit more on the experience of "letting-go" physically if we think about how our bodies situate us in a world of things. It is only natural that, in time, we become quite attached to many of these things. We may even find ourselves counting on them to tell us who we are. Some can be relatively little things, such as a souvenir, or a smoke, or a drink, or a certain kind of food. Others can be rather substantial things, such as a home, a car, a job, a wardrobe, or a plot of land. What is important is not so much whether they are little things or big things, but that, in time, we begin clinging to them.

We also live in a world of persons. Our experience with things frequently sets the tone for our experience with persons as well. Some of the persons we know become such an integral part of our lives and of our identities that we begin to treat them as though they were things which belong to us. We begin to hang onto them, in the hope that having them will make our lives meaningful.

As time goes by, we sometimes hear life asking us to "let go" of some of these things, or of some of these persons. We may find that our souvenirs are keeping us from having a future. Our experience may begin to show us that our drinking is starting to ruin our own life and that of others. The home that we have come to love so dearly may now be much too big for our dwindling family. It may become clear that it is time to let our children go their own ways and live their own lives, or that it is time to part company with a loved one, a good friend, or counselor. If we have the courage to listen closely at such times, it is as though we can hear life itself saying, from the middle of these relationships, "Let go."

At other times, the invitation to "let go" is less subtle and much less benign. Persons and things are forcibly taken from us by the circumstances of life. Our car is demolished in an accident; our home is destroyed by fire; we are fired from our job; we become disabled; our husband walks out on us; a good friend dies. When several "disasters" like these hit us at the same time, we begin to feel like Job. In fact, we may even find ourselves sitting with him in the dumps somewhere wondering what is going on. What *is* going on, whether we like it or not, is that life is emphatically telling us to "let go."

At such times, we may think that we have actually "let go" simply because circumstances have forced us to do so. However, such may not be the case at all. If we listen a little more carefully to our life, we may find that we are still clinging to these relationships in our minds and in our hearts. We may find ourselves building our lives around our memories, or living in resentment that these relationships were forcibly taken out of our hands. When we begin to realize this, we begin to hear the word "let go" resonating at still deeper levels of our lives. We begin to hear life asking us to "let go," not merely with our hands, but with our heads, with our hearts and, perhaps, with our spirit as well.

"Letting-Go" Mentally

At times, it is not our hands, but our minds, which are the focus of life's invitation to "let go." Most of us spend a good deal of time furnishing our minds with the thoughts, opinions, judgments and beliefs which help us make sense of the world in which we live. Some of this mental furniture is handed down to us from the past; some of it is borrowed from our contemporaries; some of it may be fashioned by our own experience of life. In one way or another, however, all of our mental furniture serves to remind us who we are and what our life is all about.

At times, our minds seem to be quite adequately furnished for the task of living meaningfully and we are at peace. At other times, however, our experience seems to challenge the way in which we have furnished our minds. It is as though isolated experiences begin to assault our customary way of seeing things. These are times of personal confusion and turmoil. From the middle of them, we can sometimes hear life inviting us to "let go" of some of our customary thoughts, opinions, values or beliefs.

If we think about it, most of our formal education is a controlled exercise in this experience of "letting go" mentally. Our best teachers carefully present us with facts which they hope will challenge our customary way of thinking and expand our minds. Whether we realize it or not, at the heart of these experiments in learning is an invitation to "let go" mentally. Perhaps that is why good teaching tends to generate a lot of confusion before it begins to communicate new clarity and conviction.

Life seems to teach us in very much the same way, although the experiment appears to be much less controlled. Sometimes, it is as though our experience were inviting us to "let go" of a particular piece of our mental furniture, or to rearrange the existing furniture somewhat. At other times, the invitation is much more radical; our experience starts asking us to "let go" of our basic frame of mind. For example, our whole world may have revolved, for a time, around meeting our own needs, doing our duty, making money, or some such central concern. Then our experience begins to disturb us. It begins to suggest that our lives are not to be about that at all. When we hear an invitation to "let go" at this level of our lives, we are standing on the brink of a highly personal Copernican revolution. We are being invited to empty our minds, in order to develop a new view of ourselves and of the world; we are being asked to "let go" mentally.

"Letting-Go" Emotionally

There is another, still more subtle level at which life can ask us to "let go"; it is the level of our heart. It is one thing to be asked to "let go" with our hands. It is something else to be asked to "let go" with our mind. It is something else, still, to be asked to "let go" with our heart.

If we have ever lost someone, or something, we have treasured, no one has to tell us that "out of sight" is not "out of heart." More often than not, the physical absence of the person or thing only intensifies a sort of heartfelt presence. As we listen attentively to life, however, we sometimes hear it asking us to "let go" with our heart as well. This is often a very subtle, a very delicate, and a very painful level of "letting-go."

Once a Zen Master and his disciple were making a long journey. As they approached a stream one morning, they found a young woman standing there, bewildered. She was unable to get across on her own, and did not know what to do.

The Master bowed to her, picked her up in his arms, and carried her across the stream. He put her down on the other side, bowed to her again, and continued on his way.

As night fell, the disciple broke the silence of the journey.

"Master," he said, "I have something to say to you."

"Speak," the Master replied.

"You are a Zen Master," the disciple observed. "It is
not right for you to have carried that woman in your arms."

"My son," the Master replied, "I put her down on the
other side of the stream, but you are still carrying her in
your heart."

Among other things, the disciple in this story is being asked to
"let go" with his heart. He is being invited to a change of heart. Were
he to "let go" of the young woman at that level, he might begin to
see other things differently, too. He might begin to understand what
being a Zen Master is really all about. At any rate, the story makes
clear that it is one thing for us to "let go" with our hands; it is something else to "let go" with our heart. "Letting-go" in that way is something to which life invites all of us, from time to time.

"Letting-Go" Spiritually

If we have been listening to our own lives as we have been describing these different levels of "letting-go," we are probably finding examples from our own experience beginning to multiply. That
is how it works with many of us. In fact, when we begin to realize
not only how often life has asked us to "let go," but also how often
we have actually succeeded in doing so, we begin feeling pretty good
about it. In this way, "letting-go" itself becomes another step in the
long journey of personal achievement: "I let go of this; I let go of that;
I let go of him; I let go of her; I let go of seeing things that way; I let
go of believing that; I let go of feeling angry," et cetera, et cetera.
The litany could go on and on. It often does.

If we are really honest about it, however, we may recall at
least several instances in our lives in which it was not actually "us"
who let go. In those instances we knew we were incapable of "letting-go" on our own. We had reached our limit. What happened
then surprised us. It was as though some bigger and more powerful
force than our own "I" "let go" from within us. It is often only in
retrospect that we realize this. When we do realize it, we frequently spend some time trying to name the "bigger and more
powerful force" with which we were energized at that time. We

may speak of it as "the Other," "the Not-I," "the Bigger-than-me," "the Truth," "the Mystery," "the Muse," "Yahweh," "Buddha Nature," "Life," "Grace," "Nature," "God," "Chi," "the Spirit," "Love," "the Messiah," "Tao," or many other such names. What this language is trying to describe is a personal contact with a Reality which is bigger and more powerful than our individual self. It points to a personal experience of the fact that our spirit is not an island: it is a bridge to a whole new world of more-than-personal energy and experience.

On the one hand, experiences of this kind can be so overwhelming that we may feel as though we have been annihilated. We may actually begin speaking of "the death of my self," or of "having no self."

On the other hand, such experiences mark the very beginning of our becoming spiritually aware, for they carry with them the sense of being personally animated by a Spirit that is much bigger than our own. Basically, this is what it means to "let go" spiritually; it means to let go with a courage and a power that is bigger-than-personal. In the first instance, however, it means to "stoop down" very, very low.

The Experience of "Painful Endings"

A few years ago I visited a woman to witness the marriage of her only daughter. After the guests had gone, we sat and spoke of her failing health.

"I am dying, Fran," she confided.

"Are you ready to die?" I asked.

"Yes, I am ready," she said. "It is as though my whole life has been preparing me for it."

Then she told me that she could no longer pray all the complicated prayers which she used to love to pray. She had given them all up. The only prayer which really spoke to her now was a very simple prayer of the Psalmist. She found herself praying it all the time:

Lord, I have given up my pride
and turned away from my arrogance.

I am not concerned with great matters
or with subjects too difficult for me.

Instead, I am content and at peace.
As a child lies quietly in its mother's arms,
so my heart is quiet within me.

Israel, trust in the Lord
now and forever!

Psalm 131

This was a woman who was in touch with her life spiritually. She was now hearing the invitation to "let go" of her whole life. In a certain sense, this was not the first time she had been asked to "let go" of her whole life. On one occasion, she had "let go" of her whole way of life as a very gifted lay woman to become a nun. On another occasion, she had "let go" of her life as a nun to marry a man who seemed to need her more than the Church did. More recently, she had "let go" of her whole life as a mother and a teacher to return to the convent as an oblate. This was by no means the first time she was being asked to "let go" of her whole way of life. It was as though her whole life had been preparing her for this.

As it turned out, our conversation was something like the calm before a storm. The spiritual "letting-go" which my friend shared with me was one thing. The physical "letting-go" which she would have to do alone was something else. Yet, if I have ever met one, this was a woman with the courage to "let go."

We may not all bring the same spiritual resources which my friend brought on several occasions to the prospect of dying, but we all have to face the prospect of dying. In fact, in a certain sense, we too have to face dying several times throughout our lifetime. Becoming an adult; getting married; making a major adjustment in how we live, work, think or worship; losing a loved one; working through a divorce; entering retirement—each of these experiences of transition is, in fact, a death of a sort, and on the other side of them is a different kind of life. Living in the modern world seems to require that we live, not just one, but several lives. When we put it that way, it sounds very engaging. There is a catch, however: we cannot live several lives without dying several deaths; we cannot live several lives without having the courage to "let go" and experience the painful endings.

The Fear of "Painful Endings"

From what we have been saying, it is easy to understand why so many of us find it so hard to hear the word "let go" when it begins to resonate in our lives. Whether it be at a physical, a mental, an emotional, or a spiritual level, the word "let go" is an invitation to die, at least "a little bit." An invitation like that frightens most of us. We are afraid to die—even "a little bit." So, rather than "let go," we continue to hang onto whatever, or whomever, for dear life.

Wrapped up with the fear of death comes the fear of loss. We are naturally afraid to lose our things, our thoughts, our friends, our grip on life, or our life itself.

Together with the fear of loss comes the fear of the unknown. Who knows what is on the other side of the experience of "letting-go"? Maybe there is nothing at all on the other side of it. We may well have a sense of a promise being hidden in the invitation to "let go," but our fear of the unknown tends to make us think that what we are clinging to is much better than a promise that seems beyond our reach.

Intertwined with the fear of dying, the fear of loss, and the fear of the unknown is the fear of being depressed. If what we are really about, as Americans, is the "pursuit of happiness," then what we have to avoid, at all costs, is being depressed. For many of us, even thinking about "letting-go" is depressing.

It would make things so much easier if we could say that these many fears of the painful endings associated with "letting-go" are all unfounded. Unfortunately, there is no way that we can say that. These fears are a foretaste of what "letting-go" actually feels like. At first, "letting-go" is an experience of painful endings. It brings with it a whole spectrum of painfully mixed feelings. It feels as though we are dying. It feels like being weighed down with a tremendous sense of loss. It feels like having a vacuum where our heart used to be, or like being a zombie. It often feels like being estranged from everything and everyone, including ourself. It feels like "stooping down" lower than we have ever stooped before. It feels as though something is radically wrong with us and as if everybody knows it. In other words, it is depressing.

As if that were not enough, on top of feeling depressed we frequently feel guilty about feeling depressed. We feel it is not "nice" to be depressed. We may also have been taught that it is not right, or natural, or normal, or manly, or American, or Jewish, or Christian, or Franciscan, or whatever, to be depressed. Regardless of what we may think, however, when we start "letting-go," we start feeling depressed. It takes courage to face the fears of "painful endings" and willingly to "let go."

Now that we are somewhat attuned to what the beginnings of the experience of "letting-go" sound like on the channel of our personal experience, we can listen to how the same experience sounds on the more-than-personal channel of messianic experience.

2. Channel Two: The Messianic Experience of "Letting-Go"

Our original version of the mountain climber story is thoroughly modern and very American. It pictures the mountain climber as a rugged individual who is all alone in an impossible situation. There is some truth to this, since that is often how it feels. It feels as though we were all alone with no company, no support, and, above all, no one to model what "letting-go" in this situation could possibly mean. This is a thoroughly modern and a very American picture.

The Bible presents a very different picture of the situation. It sees the whole world to be climbing the same mountain and to be stuck in the same predicament. From the biblical point of view, our original version of the mountain climber story is fine, as far as it goes. The trouble is, it does not go far enough; it only tells half the story. Perhaps that is one of the reasons why it is sometimes hard for us to tune in to Channel Two. At any rate, if we listen very closely, Channel Two gives us a very different version of our mountain climber story:

> . . . "Of course I can help you," the voice answered. "Just do as I say."

"I'll do anything you say, if only you will help me," the climber replied.

Then the voice said, "Let go."

For a long while the mountain climber was silent. He couldn't believe his ears. Then he started looking around. He noticed that he was not the only one hanging onto a tree. There were people from every time and place stuck on this mountain just as he was. Nearby, he recognized Abraham, and Moses, and Jeremiah and the Psalmist. Next to them was the Baptizer, and Jesus, and Paul, together with a host of prophets, apostles, and celebrated biblical women.

"Did you hear what the Lord said?" the mountain climber called out. "Let go! He must think I'm crazy. What is he talking about?"

The mountain climber watched in disbelief as, one by one, those who were with him let go and disappeared from his view.

Once again he began to feel all alone. "Well," he thought, "at least I'll be in good company."

Then he let go.

The Messianic Community

The biblical perspective makes a world of difference in our approach to the mountain climber story. It provides the mountain climber not only with company in his misery, but also with an encouraging example in his dilemma. This perspective can also make a world of difference in how we approach the Bible itself. Many of us approach the Bible as though it were a self-contained book, just like most any other book. We take it off a shelf and expect it to speak to us as soon as we start reading it. When it fails to live up to our expectations, we may find ourselves saying something like,

"Why does God no longer speak to his People?"

If we were to put that question to a Rabbi, he might tell us that it is not that God no longer speaks to his People, but that we had not yet stooped down low enough to listen. But if he saw that we had, in fact, stooped down low enough to be listening to life with all our heart, he might say something like:

"Where are his People? All I see is you."

Once again, a strange rabbinic reply. It strikes us as strange because it is pointing to a very different way of approaching the Bible. It is suggesting that we approach the Bible not merely as a book among many other books, but as the family journal of a messianic community. In that case, we do not find this book on a shelf. We find it in the lap of a worshiping community as it celebrates its messianic lifeline. To read the Bible from this perspective is always to be mindful of the fact that it was a worshiping messianic community that wrote it, and that it is within such a community that it speaks most clearly. It is to be personally aware that no one really reads the Bible alone. Whether we realize it or not, whenever we read the Bible, we are in "good company."

What the Rabbi may be suggesting, then, is that it is always in the context of the messianic community celebrating its lifeline that the biblical texts come alive and speak again. Apart from the presence of such a community, the biblical texts are basically out of context. Perhaps the texts no longer speak to us, because we approach them as isolated individuals. As the Rabbi says so well,

"Where are his People? All I see is you."

The Messianic Heartbeat

We may find ourselves thinking again of little Mordechai. As long as the Torah was just a book like any other book for him, it remained a closed book; it did not speak to him. What opened the book for him was hearing the heartbeat of a Rabbi who was actually living and celebrating the Word of God. It was hearing the heartbeat of a living Torah that finally unrolled the scroll and let the Scripture speak to little Mordechai.

Perhaps the story of little Mordechai wants to be taken a step further as well. The heartbeat of the Great Rabbi is not the only one that can unroll the Scripture. The heartbeat of a whole community, as it celebrates its many-faceted experience of Passingover, can let the Scripture speak again, as well. In fact, if we want to learn to listen to Channel Two, not just with our ears, but with all our heart, we have to be sensitive to the sympathetic vibrations between the heartbeat of the celebrating community and the messianic heartbeat reflected in the texts. For that reason, let us listen to the experience of "letting-go" on Channel Two in the context of the way in which the messianic community to which I belong celebrates the Passingover of Jesus.

Celebrating "Letting-Go"

For the community to which I belong, the "Day of Days" for "letting-go" is Good Friday. This day begins on Thursday evening, as we gather to celebrate Jesus' last seder supper. The Abbey church is beautifully decorated for the celebration of this very special meal.

As we gather to celebrate another Passover, our community has a certain advantage over the first disciples of Jesus. We know the whole story. It is a story we cannot forget, yet it is a story which we cannot celebrate all at once. We have to celebrate it as we have to live it—one step at a time. So it takes us three full days to celebrate the "Letting-go," the "Letting-be" and the "Letting-grow" of Passingover. We let it speak to us so that we can take it to heart, one day at a time.

For us, the story begins with a festive meal of remembering. We come together again in the hope that our celebration of the Passover will move us so deeply that it will let the Scriptures speak to us anew. We know that our celebration will begin with the experience of painful endings, but few of us come to this meal with the fear that we may get hurt. Perhaps that is one of the great advantages of our ritualized celebration of "letting-go": it lets us get in touch with the messianic energy for Passingover before we personally may have to experience the fear and the pain of it. What we try to hear most clearly, to re-enact most powerfully, and to celebrate most courageously during this first day of Passingover is the first great word of the Eighth Day of Creation: "Let go."

The "Letting-Go" of Jesus

As a faithful Jew, Jesus is in "good company" as he prepares to celebrate the Passover. He is very conscious of belonging to God's People, and of being called to take the next step in their long messianic tradition. For him, the Scriptures are not merely words that he reads; they are words that he embodies. They are part of his lifeline. After reading the Word of the Lord to them, he will tell his friends in the synagogue at Nazareth, "Today this Scripture passage is fulfilled in your hearing" (Luke 4:21).

Jesus had celebrated many Passovers with his People. These ritual celebrations served to prepare him for the very personal Passover he is now being called to celebrate. He clearly feels that his Father is asking him to "let go" of his own life, so that others may come to know what Passingover is really all about.

From the beginning of his public ministry, Jesus places himself within the whole prophetic tradition of his People by inviting them to "let go" of their own ways, so that the power of God might reign in their lives. He also goes about carefully preparing a handful of very sincere, but quite obtuse disciples, until he believes that they are finally ready to accept *how* this Reign of God in the world is actually going to come about. At what is a turning point in the first three Gospels, Jesus tests his disciples to see whether they can distinguish hearsay from the truth about his identity:

Then Jesus and his disciples went away to the villages near Caesarea Philippi. On the way he asked them, "Tell me, who do people say I am?" "Some say that you are John the Baptist," they answered; "others say that you are Elijah, while others say that you are one of the prophets." "What about you?" he asked them. "Who do you say I am?" Peter answered, "You are the Messiah." Then Jesus ordered them, "Do not tell anyone about me."

Mark 8:27–30

So much for the good news. Now Jesus feels free to begin telling his disciples what being the Messiah actually means.

Then Jesus began to teach his disciples: "The Son of Man must suffer much and be rejected by the elders, the chief priests, and the teachers of the Law. He will be put to death, but three days later he will rise to life." He made this very clear to them. So Peter took him aside and began to rebuke him. But Jesus turned around, looked at his disciples, and rebuked Peter. "Get away from me, Satan." he said. "Your thoughts don't come from God but from man!"

Mark 8:31–33

Peter is clearly trying to talk Jesus out of "letting-go." In so many words he is saying, "I'll be damned if you'll let go like that!" This reaction sums up not only the depth of Peter's love for Jesus, but also his personal expectations of the Messiah. Despite the harsh reprimand from Jesus, this reaction continues to be Peter's response to the prospect of a crucified Messiah, right up until the end. He will not let go of Jesus; and he will not let go of his notion of what being the Messiah means.

Jesus, for his part, has another way of expressing his love. As the time of his own Passingover draws near, he gathers his disciples together to celebrate the Passover meal. The disciples come together knowing very well what to expect. They have celebrated this meal many times before. The whole menu is carefully prescribed. So are all of the key actions that go with the meal. At this meal, the disciples have learned to expect no surprises. Yet Jesus surprises them. Right in the middle of the meal, he changes one of the traditional blessings:

And as they were eating, he took bread, and blessed, and broke it, and gave it to them, and said, "Take; this is my body." And he took a cup, and when he had given

thanks he gave it to them, and they all drank of it. And he
said to them, "This is my blood of the covenant, which is
poured out for many. Truly, I say to you, I shall not drink
again of the fruit of the vine until that day when I drink it
new in the kingdom of God."

Mark 14:22–25 (R.S.V.)

The Gospel of John describes still another way in which Jesus
surprises his disciples at this seder meal. In the middle of the meal,
he gets up from table, takes off his cloak, ties a towel around his
waist, pours water into a basin, and begins to wash and dry his disciples' feet. When he returns to table he says to his bewildered disciples:

Do you know what I have done to you?
You call me teacher and Lord;
and you are right, for so I am.
If I then, your Lord and Teacher,
have washed your feet,
you ought to wash one another's feet.
For I have given you an example,
that you also should do
as I have done to you.

John 13:13–15 (R.S.V.)

"I have given you an example." This is Jesus' masterfully gentle
way of saying "get in."

In the community to which I belong, these two signs of the Special Blessing and the Washing of Feet are taken as Jesus' last Will
and Testament. They mark the focal point of our celebration of "Holy
Thursday." Our first two Scripture readings describe the original
Passover meal (Exodus 12:1–8, 11–14) and what Jesus did as he celebrated his last seder (1 Corinthians 11:23–26). Then the above passage from the Gospel of John is solemnly sung by one of the priests,
while the Abbot removes his vestments, ties a towel around his waist
and re-enacts what Jesus did by washing, kissing and drying the feet
of twelve members of the community.

In a very festive way, the Abbot then blesses the bread and the cup just as Jesus did, and distributes them to the members of the community. "The Body and Blood of Christ," he says, as he hands us the Bread and the Cup. "Amen," so be it, we reply, as we eat and drink.

These powerful symbols of the Washing of Feet and the Special Blessing of Food let the Scriptures speak to us again through our own actions. They let us re-enact the "letting-go" of Jesus and express our willingness to "get in" with him—at least symbolically.

The Celebration of Painful Endings

The celebration of Holy Thursday evening ends as no other Eucharistic meal throughout the year ends. As the community stands in silence, the ministers dim the bright lights of the church and strip the altar of the flowers, the candles, the crucifix, and the special table cloth which adorned it. They remove the Blessed Bread from the tabernacle in which we usually reverence it, and leave the tabernacle, itself, empty, with its door wide open. The music stops. The singing stops. The church is silent. We will not bless the Bread again until the Third Day.

A hush comes over the community. Some wander out. Others kneel in silent prayer. The shepherd has been struck and the sheep are scattering. In the body language of our community, we are beginning to "let go" with Jesus, as a way of commemorating how he "let go" of his own life for us. "Good Friday" has begun.

Messianic Courage

There is a special intensity to the last seder of Jesus. It is clear that it is not "just another Passover meal" for him. As the meal progresses the mood becomes more somber, more apprehensive, more depressed. While the intensity of this particular Passover celebration clearly puzzles the disciples of Jesus, with the possible exception of Judas, it probably doesn't hurt them so much. It is only as Jesus begins to act out what their Passover meal had symbolized that the disciples begin to realize what was going on at table. For Jesus, re-enacting the Passover means having the courage to willingly "let go" of his own life. This is what really begins to hurt his disciples. It means that they are being invited to "let go" of their Master, and of all that they think his being the Messiah should rightfully involve. It might even mean that they are being invited to join him by "letting-go" of their own lives.

On all three counts, the disciples of Jesus resolutely refuse to "let go." For them, the seder meal is one thing; the crucifixion is something else. Part of the real pain and part of the real drama of Jesus' death lies in this stark contrast between his voluntary "letting-go" and the messianic community's failure to recognize this as an authentic celebration of the Passover. In Mark (14–15), the earliest Gospel, the drama unfolds as a dialogue between Jesus and the messianic community which reveals both the tremendous pain and the messianic courage that Jesus experiences in his ultimate "letting-go":

Jesus	*The Messianic Community*
"I tell you that one of you will betray me— one who is eating with me."	"Surely you don't mean me, do you?"
"The Son of man will die as the Scriptures say he will; but how terrible for that man who will betray the Son of Man! It would have been better for that man if he had never been born."	
"All of you will run away and leave me, for the Scripture says, 'God will kill the shepherd and the sheep will all be scattered.' "	Peter answered, "I will never leave you, even though all the rest do. I will not."
"I tell you that before the rooster crows two times tonight, you will say three times	Peter answered even more strongly, "I will never say that, even if I have to die

that you do not know me."   with you!"

"The sorrow in my heart is so great
that it almost crushes me.
Stay here
and keep watch.

"Father . . . my Father!
all things are possible for you.
Take this cup of suffering
away from me.
Yet not what I want,
but what you want."

"Simon, are you asleep?   "The man I kiss
Weren't you able to stay awake   is the one you want.
for even one hour?   Arrest him
Keep watch and pray   and take him away
that you will not fall   under guard."
into temptation.
The spirit is willing
but the flesh is weak."

" . . . But the Scriptures   "Are you the Messiah,
must come true."   the Son of the Blessed God?"

"I am . . .   "We don't need
and you will see the Son of Man any more witnesses!
seated at the right side   You heard his blasphemy.
of the Almighty   What is your decision?"
and coming   They all voted against him;
with the clouds of heaven!"   he was guilty
and should be put to death.

"I swear that
I am telling the truth!
May God punish me
if I am not!
I do not know the man
you are talking about"

Just then a rooster crowed
a second time . . .

"Crucify him!"

The notice of the accusation
against him said:
"The King of the Jews."

"He saved others,
but he cannot save himself!
Let us see the Messiah,
the king of Israel,
come down from the cross now,
and we will believe in him."

At three o'clock Jesus cried out
with a loud shout,
"Eloi, Eloi, lema sabachthani?"
which means
"My God, my God,
why did you abandon me?"

"Listen,
he is calling for Elijah!"
. . . "Wait! Let us see
if Elijah is coming
to bring him down
from the cross."

With a loud cry
Jesus died.

The army officer
who was standing there
in front of the cross
saw how Jesus died.
"This man was really
the Son of God!" he said.

The Cross, A Symbol of Messianic "Letting-Go"

As three o'clock approaches on Friday afternoon, our community gathers again for prayer. The church is still bare. As the Abbot enters to lead us in the celebration of "Good Friday," he falls flat on the floor and lies there in silent prayer for a while. Then we listen intently as the Passion of Jesus according to John is solemnly read, and respond with prayers for all the world.

Now a young woman enters the church. She wears a long white dress and carries a smoking censor. Following her are eight barefoot young men in jeans and baggy white shirts. They carry an eight foot wooden cross, veiled with a large, red drape. They carry the cross in such a way that all of us can feel the weight of it. It is a most simple, yet a most solemn procession.

As this procession slowly approaches the altar, we sing a simple chant in Greek, Latin, and English:

Holy God,
Holy Mighty One,
Holy Immortal One.
Have mercy on us.

Then the young men unveil the cross and lift it high before a part of the community. That part of the community kneels while singing.

Behold,
behold the wood of the cross
on which is hung our salvation.
O come, let us adore.

Four times this gesture is repeated until the church is a sea of faces, looking up at the cross and singing in veneration. Then the cross is laid to rest against the bare stone altar.

Before this deeply moving procession began, the cross may have become just another thing for many of us. It may have become just a piece of jewelry that we wear, or a design that we use, or a decoration that we hang on our walls. If so, this procession lets us experience the cross as much more than that. It lets us experience the cross once again as an eloquent, living symbol that can speak to us on many different levels.

On one level, the cross can speak to us as a thing. This massive, wooden cross does so eloquently. It is rugged, sturdy, and big enough to hold anyone of us.

On another level, the cross can speak to us as a curse: "God's curse rests on him who hangs on a tree" (Deuteronomy 21:23). It can symbolize all that threatens our well-being. Time has dulled this aspect of the cross for most of us. For the contemporaries of Jesus, however, the cross was the consummate curse. They abhorred it. It symbolized horrendous suffering, shame, torture, and death. For them, the cross was the antithesis of life. So strong was their abhorrence of the cross that it would be centuries before Christian communities would have the courage to portray the body of Jesus hanging on a cross. The cross can symbolize the curse.

On still another level, the cross can speak to us as a blessing: "As Moses lifted up the bronze snake on a pole in the desert, in the same way, the Son of Man must be lifted up, so that everyone who believes in him may have eternal life" (John 3:14–15). The instrument of torture itself can speak to us of healing, and the promise of a life of a different sort:

> One of the criminals hanging there hurled insults at him: "Aren't you the Messiah? Save yourself and us!" The other one, however, rebuked him saying, "Don't you fear God? You received the same sentence he did. Ours, however is only right, because we are getting what we deserve for what we did; but he has done no wrong." And he said to Jesus, "Remember me, Jesus, when you come as King!" Jesus said to him, "I promise you that today you will be in Paradise with me."
>
> *Luke 23:39–43*

As curse and blessing coincide in the symbol of the cross, the cross begins to speak to us as a paradox. It begins to tell both sides of the story at once; it symbolizes the enigma that the curse can become the blessing through the courage of "letting-go."

On yet another level, the cross can speak to us of a very special kind of person. It can speak to us of a person who has the messianic courage to embrace the paradox of the cross by willingly "letting-go":

> We despised him and rejected him;
>   he endured suffering and pain
> No one would even look at him—
>   we ignored him as if he were nothing.
> But he endured the suffering
>   that should have been ours,

the pain that we should have borne.
All the while we thought that his suffering
        was punishment sent by God.
But because of our sins he was wounded,
        beaten because of the evil we did.
We are healed by the punishment he suffered,
        made whole by the blows he received.
All of us were like sheep that were lost,
        each of us going his own way.
But the Lord made the punishment fall on him,
        the punishment all of us deserved.

Isaiah 53:4–6

If before the procession began, the cross had become merely another thing for us, it is that no longer. As we kneel together to venerate it, this rugged wooden cross speaks to us most eloquently of the whole messianic tradition of "Letting-go". It speaks to us, with awesome power, of the "letting-go" of Jesus. And it speaks to us, in a most direct way, of how we too might live our lives.

3. The Synthesis: "Letting-Go" in Stereo

A friend of mine once shared an experience with me which she said changed her whole life. As a little girl, she studied the flute with one of the foremost flutists in the country. At one of her lessons, she and her teacher were playing a duet together. All of a sudden, he stopped.

"You are listening only to yourself," he said. "You are afraid that you will make a mistake. You are worrying about how you sound, and about what I think. Now, I want you to listen to me. That's all. Do you hear? I want you to listen to me . . . Now let's try it again."

Together, they played through the whole duet, without a single interruption. When they had finished playing, the teacher turned to the little girl. There were tears in his eyes.

"For the rest of your life," he said, "remember how that felt."
The lesson was over.

The Stereo Effect

For my friend, this music lesson was a personal invitation to "let go." It invited her to move beyond a self-conscious, "monophonic," approach to making music. It did this by letting her experience the thrill of stereo: of becoming one, not only with her teacher's playing, but with the music itself. It let her realize that she did not have to fuss so much about "making music." She could simply let the music make itself. Then the music was free to be graceful, in a way that was clearly beyond her own doing. The tears of her teacher told my friend that she had learned her lesson well. What remained was for her to do, then, was to spend a lifetime putting that lesson into practice.

Something similar can happen to us if we accept the invitation to listen with all our heart, both to our own life and to the messianic heartbeat that animates the Bible. It is not a lesson in music making, however, but a lesson in living creatively. If only for a moment, we may begin to hear "let go" in living stereo. We may begin to experience a sympathetic vibration between both channels to which we are listening. It is not something that we can bring about by ourselves. It is something that just happens to us when we are listening carefully. As we begin to hear "let go" resonating in this way, it is as though our own heartbeat and the messianic heartbeat become one. It is as though our life becomes biblical, and the Bible becomes autobiographical. To experience this is to experience "the stereo effect" in our own life. It is to be tempted to "let go" and to allow our own life to become part of the messianic lifeline. It is to be tempted to "get in" and to become an active part of the Eighth Day of Creation.

By way of example, we can see this same experience of a bigger-than-personal "stereo effect" at work in the lives of Jesus and of Paul.

The "stereo effect" is certainly at work in the life of Jesus. He never tires speaking of the special, empowering relationship which he experiences between his own life and God's creative design for the world. The fact that this gets him into all kinds of trouble does not really seem to matter. He is involved in something much more important. The whole thrust of his preaching and of his ministry is to invite others to allow God's creative power to reign in their own lives, just as it does in his. Although he prefers to hide it, Jesus is keenly aware of the messianic overtones of his own way of living and dying. As his life unfolds, he begins to experience the whole Bible as autobiographical. In the end, all that he does is done "so that the Scriptures may be fulfilled . . . "

In an equally personal way, Paul picks up where Jesus left off. It is not hard to recognize Paul's experience of the "stereo effect" in his own life, as he makes statements such as:

> "I have been put to death with Christ on his cross, so that it is no longer I who live, but it is Christ who lives in me" (Galatians 2:19–20).

> "All I want is to know Christ and the power of his resurrection and to share his sufferings by reproducing the pattern of his death" (Philippians 3:10, *Jerusalem Bible*).

> "I am most happy, then to be proud of my weaknesses, in order to feel the protection of Christ's power over me. . . . For when I am weak, then I am strong" (2 Corinthians 12:9–10).

The Stereo Response

If we think about it, there is much more than the experience of the "stereo effect" going on in the example of Jesus and Paul. They are not only hearing in stereo; they are living in stereo. This is true of any other examples we could give of messianic creativity. To be complete, the stereo effect calls for a stereo response. It is one thing to hear in stereo; it is something else to respond in stereo. It is one thing to be invited to "let go"; it is something else to accept the invitation willingly. In the example of Jesus, Paul, and many, many others, it is actually through the quality of the "stereo response" which they give that we recognize the depth of the "stereo effect" which they are experiencing.

It is hard to exaggerate the importance of this difference between the stereo effect and the stereo response. Apart from a willing response to the invitation to "let go," there may be a lot of painful endings, but there can be no messianic creativity. In order to be creative, the "letting-go" must be done freely. In order to be messianic, the "letting-go" must be done in union with a more-than-personal Power. Just as the stereo effect comes from listening to life on both a personal and a more-than-personal channel, so the stereo response comes from acting simultaneously on these two channels. Just as the stereo effect cannot be heard on one channel, the stereo response cannot be given alone. This is the central paradox of messianic creativity: we are personally incapable of doing what we are clearly being invited to do.

The paradox of messianic creativity brings us back, once again, to the story of the mountain climber.

Suppose, for a moment, that the climber really wanted to "let go" but that he did not have the courage to do it. Perhaps, for the first time in his life, he was deathly afraid. Then the story could take yet another step:

> . . . "Lord," the mountain climber cried out, "are you still there?"
> "Yes," the voice replied, "I am still here."
> "Listen, Lord. I really want to let go, but I can't do it. I'm scared to death. Can you help me?"
> "Good." the voice replied. "Now we can take the next step."
> For a long time, the mountain climber was silent. Then, all of a sudden, he let go . . .

Believing as the Messianic Courage To "Let Go" in Trust

There are many ways in which we can look at believing. When life is inviting us to "let go" in stereo, however, to believe is to have courage to obey. It is to have the messianic courage to face the pain, to trust the promise, and to embrace the paradox of living creatively by freely "letting-go."

As a stereo response to the invitation to "let go," believing in no way lessens the experience of painful endings. In fact, it tends to intensify it. What believing does do is to give the pain of "letting-go" a deeper than personal meaning and direction. It places the pain of "letting-go" within the whole movement of messianic creativity.

The experience of the stereo response of believing also lends a deeper meaning to the word "let go" itself. Prior to the stereo response of a believing person, the word "let go" has a primarily passive, and a primarily negative meaning. When embodied in the stereo response of a believing person, however, the word "let go" takes on a very active and positive meaning, as well. It means actively to "en-able" the things, and persons, and thoughts, and feelings, and myriad forms of life to go. It means to set them free by giving them permission to go. In an even more basic sense, it means willingly to allow a more-than-personal Power to begin to work with us to transform our own lives and the shape of the world in which we live. To "let go" in this way is to begin to play a most active, and a most personal, part in the dawning of the Eighth Great Day of Creation.

There are two little Hebrew words which sum up all that we have said about the "stereo response" to the invitation to "let go." They are, perhaps, the two most creative words in the Bible. They are "*Amen*" and "*Alleluia.*"

When life is asking us to "let go," to believe means to have the courage to say "*Amen*": "so be it." It means to have the messianic courage to say "Yes" with all one's life, to becoming a channel for God's creative designs.

At such a time, to believe also means to have the courage to say "*Alleluia*": "praise God." It means to have the courage to give praise to the Creative Power that animates us, as we find ourselves doing what we know we cannot do on our own. As a rule, the "*Alleluia*" tends to arrive a bit late in the experience of painful endings. When it does arrive, it frequently arrives quite tentatively, as a whisper, and often in a minor key. It is praise, to be sure, but it is praise with a heavy heart, for our heart hangs heavy when it is "letting-go." However, if we continue to respond, on every level of our lives, to the invitation to "let go," our "*Alleluia*" becomes much stronger, as it transposes itself, in a most surprising way, into a major key. Then we may find ourselves, together with the whole messianic tradition, not just enduring, but actually celebrating, the experience of "let-ting-go" and actually praising God from the middle of it.

How a response as joyous as *"Alleluia"* can be so intimately re-lated to the experience of painful endings will become clearer when we consider the next step in the Art of Passingover. Even before that, however, *"Amen"* and *"Alleluia"* sum up, in two little words, the creative fidelity which is involved in "letting-go" in stereo.

In this chapter, we have been reflecting on "letting-go" as both a personal and a messianic experience of painful endings. We have described believing as the "stereo response" through which the per-sonal and the messianic become one. This experience of "letting-go" is the first key action involved in the Art of Passingover. It is the first great step toward ushering in the Eighth Day of Creation. With this in mind, we can now turn our attention to the second key action in-volved in the Art of Passingover, namely, to "letting-be."

Chapter 4

Letting-Be
The Experience of Awkward Inbetweens

Be still,
and know
that I am
God.
Psalm 46:11 (R.S.V.)

A while ago, we saw our mountain climber realizing that he was in good company and "letting-go." We are now in a position to realize that the story does not stop there, either. It takes yet another step:

As he fell, the mountain climber was bruised, battered, and frightened half to death. But then a strange thing began to happen. He seemed to get used to falling. His fall became increasingly graceful, and much less painful. In fact, he began to experience a kind of freedom in falling which he had never experienced in climbing.

All of a sudden, a cloud enveloped him, and he realized that he was not falling anymore. In fact, he was not moving at all. He was suspended in midair. He could not see or feel anything anymore.

"We made it, Lord!" he called out, "We made it! . . . What do I do now?"

From within the cloud, the voice replied, "Let it be."

The climber waited for a while. "But, Lord," he objected, "this is boring."

"Let it be," the voice responded.

The climber shrugged his shoulders. "I was afraid you were going to say that!"

This part of the story introduces us to the next key word in the Art of Passingover: "Let it be." It also suggests what it actually feels like to "let be." It feels like being numb, blind, half-dead, and suspended in midair. It feels like being nobody, nowhere, with nothing to do. It feels like being in limbo. To feel this way is to experience "the awkward inbetween"; it is to be invited to take the next step in the Eighth Great Day of Creation by willingly "letting-be."

The Other Side of "Letting-Go"

If we attend to our own experiences of "letting-go," what we notice, first of all, is how painful they are. For a while, our worst fears are usually realized. If we stay faithful to the experience of "letting-go," however, we often experience a certain freedom, and even joy, on the other side of it. Much to our surprise, it is as though a little *alleluia* comes tagging along, on the other side of "letting-go."

For example, suppose that we feel called to "let go" of smoking, and actually do so. At first we experience the pain of "letting-go." It may be so bad, at times, that we think we are going to die if we cannot smoke. But, we do not die. As time goes by, we get used to the pain. At first, "letting-go" seems to expand our capacity to suffer gracefully. Then, on the other side of the pain, we begin to experience the relief, the freedom, and perhaps even the joy of living without the habit of smoking. We rediscover the freshness of air, and the joy of unknown smells and tastes again. We experience a sense of independence. We come alive again.

On occasion, the joy that can come with "letting-go" is something that we will not even admit to ourselves. For example, we may have devoted a good part of our life to caring for our invalid mother. When our mother dies, we experience a great sense of loss. It is as though a part of our self has died. On many different levels, we are called to "let go" of our mother. At first, the pain of "letting-go" is very intense. Later on, however, we begin to experience a sense of relief and freedom, on the other side of the pain. A great responsibility has been taken from our shoulders. It is over, and we feel as though we are floating free again. When we realize this, we experience a sense of relief, freedom, and joy on the other side of our experience of "letting-go," and, in one form or another, an *alleluia* wells up within us, even though we may not care to admit it. This experience of the other side of "letting-go" lets us understand the paradoxical, bittersweet character of "letting-go" and that the only way to get to the other side is through the experience of painful endings.

As we experience the other side of "letting-go," we often find ourselves beginning to wonder, "What do I do now?" This question is a prelude to the experience of "letting-be," for life's unwelcome reply is frequently, "Let it be."

In order to get some sense of what the stereo response to "Let be" involves, let us listen to life, first of all, on the channel of our personal experience, and then on the channel of messianic experience.

1. Channel One: The Personal Experience of "Letting-Be" The Experience of Awkward Inbetweens

When we speak of the experience of "awkward inbetweens," we often are led back to our experience as adolescents. At that time in our lives, most of us experience and enact, in a most dramatic way, the awkward inbetween that separates being a child from being an adult. We are no longer children; we have "let go" of that. We are not yet adults. For the time being, we are clearly inbetween and it is awkward. We are full of strange energies, yet we feel as though we have nothing to do. We feel bored, restless, clumsy, lost, out of place and out of sorts. What is worse, we feel as though everybody in the world notices how awkward we are.

More often than not, this experience of the awkward inbetween invites us to a hiding place. It invites us to find someplace where we can simply "let it be" and not feel so conspicuous. Quite instinctively, we begin looking for a room of our own, an attic, a tree house, a state of mind, or some similar place apart, where we can be alone and get in touch with ourselves. Whatever its shape may be, this hiding place is a sort of cocoon in which a major mystery of growth takes place.

Few of us have to be told that experiencing the "awkward inbetween" is not limited to adolescence. It is part of changing schools, moving away, getting married, changing jobs, convalescing, deepening a relationship, getting divorced, being retired—in fact, it is part of any of the many major changes we are called to work through in our lives. At such times, we may find ourselves saying something like, "I should have gone through this in adolescence." What life seems to be teaching us, however, is that we are never too old to experience the "awkward inbetween."

Frequently, we are not the only ones who feel awkward at times such as these. Those closest to us can see that we are not ourselves. They no longer know how we are going to act, or react; they find it awkward to be around us. They often encourage us to "get away," to take a vacation, to go on a sabbatical, to make a retreat, to tour the world—in effect, to get out of their sight! Actually, this is very good advice, since it points us to socially acceptable and institutionalized ways of "going to the hiding place" without upsetting others too much. It also gives us some non-threatening words which can serve as hiding places in themselves: "get away," "vacation," "sabbatical," "retreat," "travel," "transition." When life is telling us to "let be," we often find ourselves inclined to take our friends' advice—whether we want to or not.

The Fear of "Letting-Be"

Some of us dream of having nothing to do and of being so free that we can finally do the many things we have always wanted to do but have never gotten around to doing. When we are experiencing the awkward inbetween of life, however, that dream seldom comes true. The freedom we experience at that time is more like a type of numbness. It is like the calm after the storm of "letting-go." We find ourselves relieved to have "let go" but without the heart to do anything else. At a time like that, to hear the invitation "Let be" can be extremely frightening; it raises some of our deepest fears, as we echo the mountain climber's anxious call, "What do I do now?"

Most of us are deathly afraid of losing control of our own lives. When we are experiencing the awkward inbetween, we literally do not know what is going on, and we do not know what to do about it. We are out of control; for most of us, to let that situation continue is very frightening.

Many of us are also afraid of being useless or unproductive. In this culture, we are what we do. One of the first things we ask one another when we meet is, "What are you doing these days?" For most of us, it is a nightmare to think of having to respond, "Who, me? Well . . . I . . . ah . . . I'm just being!" No matter how hard we have worked in the past, most of us are afraid of lying fallow.

Hand in hand with the fear of being useless comes the fear of being bored. If anything can be said about our life in the modern world, it is that it is stimulating. In fact, our life can be so stimulating that we equate living with being excited. Against such a background, "let be" sounds frightfully boring.

Another deep-seated fear which we have is the fear of having no future. Many of us draw our energy and our patience from our vision of what will come to be. The experience of the "awkward inbetween," however, is an eclipse of the future. Our past is over. Our future is out of sight. All that we have to go on is what is. To hear "let be" at this time is to be asked to honor a most unwelcome present without knowing what will be. For most of us, that is very frightening.

We also have a natural fear of our inner shadow. The initial boredom involved in "letting-be" often gives way to a sort of bombardment from within. We are visited by the most threatening images of our own inadequacy, weakness, and inner ugliness. These inner shadows may come while we are asleep, in the form of dreams or nightmares, or they may also come while we are awake, in the form of memories, thoughts, feelings, moods, or fantasies. In whatever form they come, they often come with a power and a reality that can overwhelm us and frighten us half to death. "Who needs this?" is a very natural reaction to this sort of bombardment from within, and "let it be" is no consolation at all.

Underneath all of these fears, we seem to be afraid of our inner loneliness. As the bombardment from within, which is involved in "letting-be," quiets down, it frequently takes us to an experience of

silence and nothingness that is even more intense than our original
experience of boredom was. We now begin to experience our ultimate solitude, our ultimate, inalienable loneliness. This is, perhaps,
the most frightening experience of all.

> . . . the Master stopped, again. "What do you hear, now?"
> he asked . . . The old man nodded. And continued on his
> way.

"The Journey into Silence" comes to mind again as we describe
our fear of "letting-be," since it is a journey which passes through
these experiences. All along the way, the Master's gentle nod is his
way of saying, "That is how it is. Let it be."

It would be a relief were we able to say that the fears we have
just described are illusions. They are not, however. They are a very
real part of the experience of "letting-be" and a very real indication
of what courage it takes to listen to life from within the experience
of the "awkward inbetween."

The Flight from "Letting-Be"

In light of our fear of "letting-be," it is not hard to imagine a very
different ending to the story of "The Journey into Silence":

> . . . Then, the Master stopped again. "What do you hear,
> now?" he asked.
>   "Master, I hear the thunder in the distance, and it
> frightens me to death!" the disciple replied.
>   The old man nodded. And continued on his way.
>   The disciple called out after him. "Master," he cried,
> "I can take it no more. Wisdom is too far away. I am going
> back to where I was."
>   The old man nodded. And continued on his way.
> Alone.

Rather than let his fear be, the disciple now opts to run away
from it. In doing so, he follows a well-worn path of the flight from

"letting-be." That flight can take many forms. The form it takes for the disciple, here, is to run back to what he had once let go of. He did not like where he was; he did not know where he was going; so he turned back to what he had known before. This is the "back to Egypt" response to "let be"; it is a very common form of flight from "letting-be."

Another form of flight from "letting-be" is fussing around. We do not know what to do in the awkward inbetween and we are afraid just to "let it be." So we start running around, aimlessly, doing anything and everything, in a sort of frenzied panic. This is the direct opposite of what "letting-be" requires. "Letting-be" says, "Don't just do something! Sit there!" Fussing around says, "Don't just sit there! Do something!" By fussing around, we keep ourselves busy so that we do not have to enter the silence and listen to what life might have to say to us at a deeper level.

Still another way in which we flee from "letting-be" is to blame someone else for bringing us to the place of awkward inbetween. This response can become a very vicious game. The game is called "Get the leader" or "Find the scapegoat." It is often played by lashing out at those who are closest to us, and who are frequently most concerned about our welfare. By playing "Get the leader" or "Find the scapegoat," we distract ourselves from having to listen to "let be."

In light of this way of fleeing from "letting-be," we can easily imagine the disciple in our story cursing the old man for leading him to such frightful places. We may even be able to recall the suffering faces of friends, parents and leaders we have known, who were the unwitting, and unhappy, objects of this form of flight from "letting-be."

The Courage To "Let Be"

Running away, fussing, and blaming are just three of the many ways in which we can flee from the invitation to "let be." They show how much courage it takes to listen to our life as it speaks to us from the experience of awkward inbetweens. If we listen to it carefully, the following story brings the same message home:

There once was a hermit who lived in the hills outside of a little town. He was revered by all the townspeople as a holy man.

One day, a young girl, who lived in the town, was found to be pregnant. Her father was furious. He insisted that she tell him who was the father of the baby. The girl resisted for as long as she could, but finally she admitted, "It is the holy man who lives in the hills."

The father immediately took the baby and went out to see the hermit. "You hypocrite!" he shouted. "This is your baby. You care for it!"

"Is that how it is?" the hermit replied. So he took the baby and began to care for it.

From then on, whenever the hermit would come down into the town to beg, he would carry the baby with him. The townspeople cursed him, mocked him, and gave him next to nothing to feed himself and the child.

Several years went by. Finally, the young girl could bear it no longer. "Father," she said, "I have lied to you. The holy man is not the father of my baby." Then she told him who the father really was.

The girl's father was overwhelmed with grief and shame. He went out to see the hermit. "Please forgive me," he said. "I have done you a terrible wrong. You are not the father of this child."

"Is that how it is?" the hermit replied. Then he gave the baby back to the girl's father with his blessing.

Depending on our point of view, this can be either a "wisdom story" or a "stupidity story."

If we have listened to "let be" in our own lives on several occasions, this story tends to be a wisdom story. It celebrates the courage of a person who has learned to let life be. The holy man in this story is someone who has "let go" of his good reputation. He does not defend or justify himself. He does not blame the little girl or contradict the irate father. With knowing compassion, he simply lets life be. He has the extraordinary courage to affirm what "is" so that, in time, it may take its next step and become what it is really meant to be.

On the other hand, if we find it hard to listen to "let be" in our own lives, this will probably be just another "stupid story." In fact, it might strike us as so stupid that we wonder why anyone would go to the trouble of telling it. If it is told very well, however, it can start to haunt us—especially when our own lives are inviting us to "let be."

"Is that how it is?"—the holy man has clearly committed himself to living with this question and with all of its consequences. It takes a lot of courage to do that. Perhaps that is why we tend to explore so many roads which head in the opposite direction from "letting-be."

The escape routes from "letting-be" are not one way roads, however. They go in both directions, and we can always make a "U-turn." We can always reverse our direction and return to the place where we can again hear the creative word "let be." Making such a turn requires a good deal of courage in itself. It can be made much easier, however, if we have the good fortune to know someone who resolutely lets life be. The disciple in "The Journey into Silence" has had the good fortune of knowing someone like that, so that we can easily imagine him returning to his Master and the story taking still another step:

> After several days, the disciple began to regret that he had left his Master. "I will never get anywhere, following this way," he said to himself. Then he turned around, and set out to find the old man.
>
> After a long search, the disciple came upon his Master. Without making a sound, he fell in behind the old man, happy that his arrival went unnoticed. For six full days, he followed along in this way.
>
> As the seventh day dawned, the Master stopped. "What do you hear now?" he asked.
>
> "I hear the babbling of the brook," the disciple replied, "and it comforts me."
>
> The old man nodded. And continued on his way . . .

In listening to the experience of "letting-be" on the channel of our personal experience, we have found that it is a sometimes frightening experience of the "awkward inbetween" which takes considerable courage to experience fully. Now we can begin listening to how "letting-be" sounds on the more-than-personal channel of messianic experience.

2. Channel Two: The Messianic Experience of Letting-Be

In order to hear what the "letting-be" which is at the heart of the messianic experience sounds like, we have to listen to more than just the words of the Bible. We have to listen to the silence between the words, and to the symbols the words become, as they allude to an experience so rich that no words can express it fully.

Listening to Silence

First of all, we have to listen to silence, for the messianic experience of "letting-be" is often carried by a most eloquent silence.

Let us listen to another journey into silence, and to the silence at the center of it, as the Psalmist prays his way through one of the most desolating experiences of his life:

> My God, my God, why have you abandoned me?
> I have cried desperately for help
>   but still it does not come.
> During the day I call to you, my God
>   but you do not answer;
> I call at night, but get no rest.
> But you are enthroned as the Holy One,
>   the one whom Israel praises.
> Our ancestors put their trust in you;
>   they trusted you, and you saved them.
> They called to you and escaped from danger;
>   they trusted you and were not disappointed.
>
> But I am no longer a man; I am a worm
>   despised and scorned by everyone!
> All who see me make fun of me;
>   they stick out their tongues and shake their heads.

"You relied on the Lord," they say,
    "Why doesn't he save you?"
If the Lord likes you,
    why doesn't he help you?"

It was you who brought me safely through birth,
    and when I was a baby, you kept me safe.
I have relied on you since the day I was born,
    and you have always been my God.
Do not stay away from me!
    Trouble is near, and there is no one to help.

Many enemies surround me like bulls;
    they are all around me,
    like fierce bulls from the land of Bashan.
They open their mouths like lions,
    roaring and tearing at me.

My strength is gone,
    gone like water spilled on the ground.
All my bones are out of joint;
    my heart is like melted wax.
My throat is as dry as dust,
    and my tongue sticks to the roof of my mouth.
You have left me for dead in the dust.

A gang of evil men is around me;
    like a pack of dogs they close in on me;
    they tear at my hands and feet.
All my bones can be seen.
    My enemies look at me and stare.
They gamble for my clothes
    and divide them among themselves.

O Lord, don't stay away from me!
    Come quickly to my rescue
Save me from the sword;
    save my life from these dogs.

Rescue me from these lions;
>   I am helpless before these wild bulls.

(S-i-l-e-n-c-e)

I will tell my people what you have done;
>   I will praise you in their assembly:
"Praise him, you servants of the Lord!
Honor him, you descendants of Jacob!
Worship him, you people of Israel!
He does not neglect the poor
>   or ignore their suffering;
>   he does not turn away from them,
>   but answers when they call for help."

In the full assembly I will praise you
>   for what you have done;
>   in the presence of those who worship you
>   I will offer the sacrifices I promised.
The poor will eat as much as they want;
>   those who come to the Lord will praise him.
May they prosper forever!
All nations will remember the Lord.
>   From every part of the world
>   they will turn to him;
>   all races will worship him.
The Lord is king, and he rules the nations.

All proud men will bow down to him;
>   all mortal men will bow down before him.
Future generations will serve him;
>   men will speak of the Lord
>   to the coming generation.
People not yet born will be told:
>   "The Lord saved his people."

Psalm 22

What happens, within the silence at the center of this psalm to
account for such a radical change of mood? What happens, within

that awkward pause, to transform such fear and suffering into such courage and joy? The Psalmist does not tell us; it is the silence which speaks to us of "letting-be."

For yet another example, let us listen to the silence, at the heart of Paul's proclamation of the Good News:

> And after they had done everything that the Scriptures say about him, they took him down from the cross and placed him in a tomb.
>
> (S-i-l-e-n-c-e)
>
> But God raised him from death, and for many days he appeared to those who had traveled with him from Galilee to Jerusalem. They are now witnesses for him to the people of Israel. And we are here to bring the Good News to you: what God promised our ancestors he would do, he has now done for us, who are their descendants, by raising Jesus to life. As it is written in the second Psalm,
>
> 'You are my Son;
> today I have become your Father.'
> *Acts 13:28–33*

What happens in the silence at the center of this preaching to transform such bad news into such good news? What happens within that tomb, to transform such a defeat into such a victory? Paul does not tell us; it is the silence which speaks of "letting-be."

Listening to Symbols

In order to hear what the "letting-be" at the heart of the messianic experience sounds like, we have to learn to listen, not only to silence, but to symbols as well. Three of the most eloquent symbols through which the Bible speaks of "letting-be" are the desert, the Sabbath, and the vigil. Once we learn to listen to these symbols, many of the biblical texts become surprisingly eloquent; they begin to speak for themselves.

The Symbol of the Desert

For the people who wrote the Bible, the desert is a hard fact of life. It is a useless, barren, arid, desolate, seemingly godforsaken wasteland, which is inhabited by savage beasts and evil spirits. To get lost out there is certain death.

The desert is much more than a hard fact of life for the people who wrote the Bible, however. As they recognize the desert for what it is, it becomes much more for them. From the Exodus experience onward, the desert becomes a symbol of the messianic relationship with God, and it begins to speak about that relationship in many different ways.

On one level, the desert speaks of the ultimate ordeal; it speaks of the experience of facing pain, temptation, suffering, desolation, and even death in the wilderness. It speaks as *the* place apart. It speaks of the deepest personal longing for God: "O God, you are my God whom I seek; for you my flesh pines and my soul thirsts like the earth, parched, lifeless and without water" (Psalm 63:2). It also speaks of the experience of personal desertedness: "I will make her like the desert, reduce her to an arid land, and slay her with thirst" (Hosea 2:5). It speaks, as well, of the greatest temptation: the temptation to desert God. As the people get tired of wandering in the desert, after having "let go" of Egypt, they not only begin to play "Back to Egypt" and "Get the Leader," but they also begin to play "Do It Yourself" and "Make Your Own God." The Psalmist sums up God's reaction to such infidelity when he writes:

Listen today to what he says:
"Don't be stubborn, as your ancestors were at Meribah,
     as they were that day in the desert at Massah.
There they put me to the test and tried me,
     although they had seen what I did for them.
For forty years I was disgusted with those people.
I said, 'How disloyal they are!

They refuse to obey my commands.'
I was angry and made a solemn promise:
'You will never enter the land
where I would have given you rest.' "

Psalm 95:7–11

The desert speaks not only of the ultimate ordeal, but also of the ultimate promise. The mountain of God is in the middle of the desert. People are called into the desert to come to know and worship God in that seemingly desolate place (Exodus 5:1–3). The desert is a place of meeting; it is a hiding place where "angels wait," new perspectives emerge, new possibilities are perceived, and remarkable transformations take place. It is in the desert that Abraham becomes a Patriarch, that Moses becomes a leader, that the Jews become a People, that Elijah meets his God, that the Baptizer finds his vocation, and that Jesus overcomes the Evil One. The desert is a place of repentance, discovery, Sabbath, and renewal to which the messianic community is called—not just once and for all—but again and again:

So I am going to take her into the desert again;
there I will win her back
with words of love.
I will give back to her the vineyards she had
and make Touble Valley a door of hope.
She will respond to me there
as she did when she was young,
when she came from Egypt. . . .
Israel, I will make you my wife;
I will be true and faithful;
I will show you constant love and mercy
and make you mine forever,
I will keep my promise and make you mine,
and you will acknowledge me as Lord.

Hosea 2:14–15; 19–21

As it continues to speak of the promise, the desert becomes an eloquent symbol of the ultimate passageway. It is the unlikely, yet

God-made, pathway to the Promised Land. It is the land of inbetween. Only God knows the way through it. It is he who calls persons
into the desert, not only to liberate them, to meet them, and to test
them, but also personally to lead them through it to the other side.
The dry way through the sea, the guiding column of cloud, the pillar
of fire, the mountaintop teachings, the healing sign of the snake, the
nourishing manna, quail, and water from the rock, are not meant for
the first Exodus experience alone. They are meant for every subsequent desert journey. They are eloquent symbols for the many ways
by which God leads survivors through the desert with such subtlety
that no one sees his footprints. Perhaps that is why the messianic
community keeps its eye peeled on those who come out of the desert. It is convinced that, if they made it through, they must have
been led by God.

In speaking to us as a symbol of the ultimate ordeal, promise
and passageway, the desert speaks to us as a supreme paradox. It
speaks, at one and the same time, as a place of death and a place of
life; as a place of disenchantment and a place of discovery; as a place
of temptation and a place of blessing; as a place of betrayal and a place
of fidelity; as a place of barrenness and a place of fertility; as a place
of rest and a place of passage. In this way, the desert symbolizes the
real complexity of the messianic relationship with God, and the many
faces of the experience of the "awkward inbetween." It is a most paradoxical symbol of a most paradoxical experience.

The Symbol of the Sabbath

For the people who wrote the Bible, the Sabbath is "a day
apart"—a very different day. It is a day so different that it transforms
and animates all other days. It is a day of rest, a day of meeting, and
a day of blessing. It is a day of distancing ourself from the everyday
concerns of the workaday world, and simply being in admiration of
the world and its Creator. It is a quiet day in which to listen to the
Word of God anew and take it to heart.

The Bible traces the origin of this day backward through the
desert of Sinai and Mosaic Covenant, to the cosmic desert in
which God first worked and to the covenant he made with all of
creation:

Observe the Sabbath and keep it holy. You have six days in which to do your work, but the seventh day is a day of rest dedicated to me. On that day no one is to work—neither you, your children, your slaves, your animals, nor the foreigners who live in your country. In six days I, the Lord, made the earth, the sky, the seas, and everything in them, but on the seventh day I rested. That is why I, the Lord, blessed the Sabbath and made it holy.

Exodus 20:8–11

The Sabbath is a day of wonder. It is a day of entering into the creative rest of God. It is a day of imitating God's creative rhythm by letting all of creation be.

From a biblical point of view, all creative activity leads to this most creative day:

And God said, "Let there be . . .
   and there was . . .
And God said, "Let there be . . .
   And it was so . . .
And God said, "Let there be . . .
   And it was so . . .
   And it was so . . .
   And it was so . . ."

So God blessed the seventh day and hallowed it, because on it he rested from all the work he had done in creation.

Genesis 1:3–2:3 (R.S.V.)

The Bible sees all truly creative activity flowing through, and from, this most creative day as well. In spite of its apparent lack of activity, the Sabbath is a supremely creative day. It is a day on which persons allow God himself to work creatively within them. The Sabbath is a day of most active idleness. It is the supreme day of the messianic Covenant; it is the day of "letting-be."

Judging from all the laws which were later made to protect the symbol of the Sabbath, the early Jews did not find it any easier than we do to "let go" of our own work, and to let God's work within us

be. They seem to have found "letting-be" just as awkward and as te-
dious as we do. The Sabbath laws can be seen to enumerate the many
ways people had found of "fussing around" instead of "letting-be."
Such "fussing around" on the Sabbath was not taken lightly, however: it was punishable by death:

> The Lord commanded Moses to tell the people of Israel,
> "Keep the Sabbath, my day of rest, because it is a sign be-
> tween you and me for all time to come, to show that I, the
> Lord, have made you my own people. You must keep the
> day of rest, because it is sacred. Whoever does not keep it,
> but works on that day, is to be put to death . . . "
>
> *Exodus 31:12–14*

From one point of view, to impose such a severe penalty for
breaking the Sabbath seems like extreme legalism. From another
point of view, however, it highlights the supreme importance of the
experience of the Sabbath. The Sabbath is the soul of Israel. It is a
day which says that there is something to be learned by "letting-be"
which can be learned in no other way. It is a day which says that there
can be no spiritual growth without the creative rhythm of rest and
work, and without the intensified contact with the creativity of God,
which the Sabbath rest can provide. From this point of view, the
death penalty which the law imposes may not be legalistic at all. It
may just be the legal expression of the penalty which life itself eventually imposes on a Sabbathless life.

Over time, the laws which were designed to protect the nature of the Sabbath become so numerous, so complex, and so rigid
that they risk stifling the spirit of the Sabbath itself. It is toward
reviving that spirit that Jesus steadfastly points in the instances in
which he and his disciples break the laws of the Sabbath to do
something creative (see Mark 2:23–28; John 5). Jesus puts it this
way: "The Sabbath was made for man, not man for the Sabbath"
(Mark 2:27).

At a later date, the Sabbath way of entering into the Lord's creative rest is seen to mirror the God-given covenant and the creativity
not only of the messianic community, but of the ultimate Promised
Land, as well (Hebrews 3–4).

In more ways than one, the Sabbath is a very powerful symbol of the messianic experience of "letting-be."

The Symbol of the Vigil

Another great symbol of the messianic experience of "letting-be" is a very special type of waiting and watching.

For many of us, waiting and watching is something to be avoided. It is an exercise in boredom—a way of killing time. We associate it with a sort of mindless standing in line at a bus stop or a checkout counter.

The messianic experience of waiting and watching is very different from this. It is filled with a passion for Passingover. It is animated by a heartfelt longing and hungering for deliverance, and justice, and truth, and love, and meaning, and life, and God. It is a creative attentiveness which, in time, allows persons to hear, and see and recognize what would otherwise go unheard, unseen and unrecognized.

This is the kind of watching and waiting the Psalmist is talking about when he prays:

> I wait eagerly for the Lord's help,
>   and in his word I trust.
> I wait for the Lord
>   more eagerly than watchmen
>   wait for the dawn—
> than watchmen wait for the dawn.
> *Psalm 130:5–7*

This is the kind of watching and waiting the author of the Second Letter of Peter is talking about, when he tells his persecuted community:

> So we are even more confident of the message proclaimed by the prophets. You will do well to pay attention to it, because it is like a lamp shining in a dark place until the Day dawns and the light of the morning star shines in your hearts.
> *2 Peter 1:19*

This is the kind of watching and waiting the Israelites do as they eat the Passover lamb and wait for the Lord Himself to liberate them (Exodus 12). It is the kind of watching and waiting the prophet Ezekiel does as he stands staring at a desert full of dry bones, wondering whether the Lord will bring them to life again (Ezekiel 37:1–14). It is the kind of watching and waiting the child Samuel does as he rises from sleep to say to the Lord, "Speak; your servant is listening" (1 Samuel 3:9). It is the kind of watching and waiting Elijah does, as he stands on Mount Sinai through a hurricane, an earthquake and a blazing fire, until he recognizes his Lord in a tiny whispering sound (1 Kings 19). It is the kind of watching and waiting the beloved does, as she waits for her lover: "I slept, but my heart was awake. Hark! My beloved is knocking . . . " (Songs of Songs 5:2 R.S.V.). When the Baptizer sends some disciples to ask Jesus, "Are you the one John said was going to come or should we expect someone else?" (Matthew 11:3), they are speaking for centuries of this very special kind of passionate, messianic watching and waiting. This is the type of messianic watchfulness which Jesus enjoins on his disciples, as he tells them:

> "Be on watch, be alert, for you do not know when the time will come. It will be like a man who goes away from home on a trip and leaves his servants in charge, after giving to each one his own work to do and after telling the doorkeeper to keep watch. Watch, then, because you do not know when the master of the house is coming—it might be in the evening or at midnight or before dawn or at sunrise. If he comes suddenly, he must not find you asleep. What I say to you, then, I say to all: Watch!"
>
> *Mark 13:33–37*

Not much later, Jesus agonizes through just this kind of vigil, while his disciples fall asleep (Mark 14:32–42).

It may be hard for us, at first, to see the connection between this passionate kind of waiting and our traditional religious vigils. We often schedule vigils so that no one will lose any sleep. We also try to keep them short so that no one will get bored. In spite of this well intentioned planning, we still get bored, and still find ourselves dozing during vigils. At times the conventional religious vigil makes standing at the bus stop or the checkout counter seem interesting.

Keeping vigil was not always that way, however. Long before it became a religious tradition, it was a religious passion. People began to vigil, not because it was scheduled or customary, but because they were so threatened, or so frightened, or so hopeful, or so filled with longing, or so excited by what was starting to stir in them that they could not sleep. Apart from a personal experience of this kind of vigilance, much of what the Bible has to say about watching and waiting is wasted on us.

Once again, the Psalmist can be our teacher. He speaks from an intensely personal experience of vigiling as these most soul-searching questions keep him awake:

> I spend the night in deep thought;
> I meditate, and this is what I ask myself:
> "Will the Lord always reject us?
> Will he never again be pleased with us?
> Has he stopped loving us?
> Does his promise no longer stand?
>
> Has God forgotten to be merciful?
> Has anger taken the place of his compassion?"
> Then I said, "What hurts me most is this—
> that God is no longer powerful."
>
> I will remember your great deeds, Lord;
> I will recall the wonders you did in the past
> I will think of all that you have done;
> I will meditate on all your mighty acts.
> *Psalm 77:6–12*

The vigil is a messianic way of facing life. It is a biblical symbol for letting all of life be: the problems, the memories, the fears, the pains, the anxieties, the persons, the situations, the desires, the beliefs, the doubts, the hopes, the dreams, the emptiness—above all, the emptiness. It is a symbol for a passionate kind of waiting that lets darkness be until it bears the light; that lets silence be until it breathes a Word; that lets solitude be until it reveals community; that lets the nothingness be until it is transformed.

Celebrating "Awkward Inbetweens"

The silence, the desert, the Sabbath, and the vigil all speak to the messianic community of the experience "letting-be" and "awkward inbetweens." The community does not just listen to this experience, however, it celebrates it. It does not just endure the silence, the desert, the Sabbath, and the vigil, it celebrates them as ways in which it experiences anew the power of God and its own identity.

For the messianic community to which I belong, the silence, the desert, the Sabbath, and the vigil all come together in the one great day, which we call "Holy Saturday"—the Great Sabbath. This is a day which begins as the sun sets on Friday and continues until the sun rises on the Lord's Day. It is a desert day, a day of watching and waiting.

If we were to ask what the community does to mark this great day, we would have to say, "Nothing." It is a day without liturgy. The church is unadorned. The altar is stripped. The tabernacle is bare. We do not celebrate the Eucharist. We do not eat much. We do not talk much. We do gather together to listen to the Lamentations of Jeremiah and to affirm our hope in a new day, but, for the most part, we simply watch and wait, and stay still. We simply "let be."

In a very real way, the life of our whole community, at this time, is reflected in this very different day. Over twenty years ago, our spiritual leaders convened in the Second Vatican Council and reminded us that we are a Pilgrim People. We took heart in that reminder and headed joyously into the desert to worship God as he wishes, and to be renewed. Now, we are beginning to realize what being a Pilgram People actually involves. We are beginning to realize that we are only at the beginning of a period of spiritual renewal which may take a century or two. Many of us find that disheartening and long for quicker results, easier ways and better times. Given this situation, it is more important for us these days than ever to celebrate the Great Sabbath, and to learn to "let be" in God's good time.

There is a tall wooden cross on top of the hill which faces our Abbey church. It is there all year around, but it fits in so well among the trees that it goes hardly noticed. On the Great Sabbath, it stands out. As the sun sets on Friday night, we light a torch before it and keep the torch burning until Sunday morning. All day Saturday, people leave the road and climb up the hill to the cross. They kneel or sit around it, saying their prayers. Then they wander off, silently. It is that kind of day.

For us, the cross symbolizes the messianic "letting-go," but that is not all it symbolizes; it also symbolizes the messianic "letting-be." In spirit, we spend this Great Sabbath in the shadow of the cross. We spend it at the sealed door of an ancient tomb, wondering, "Can anything good can come of this?"

After nightfall on Saturday, we gather again in the darkness of the Abbey church to celebrate the Vigil of Vigils. We wait in silence for what seems to be a very long time. Then a young man carries a flaming torch through the church to the altar, where the Abbot stands waiting. The torch both frightens and delights us. It could easily set the church on fire. But it can also illuminate the Word of God and the darkness of our lives. Ever so carefully, the young man lights the Passover Candle with the torch as we sing, again and again, "Light of Christ," "Thanks be to God." Then the flame is passed from the Passover Candle to the candles which each of us holds, and the church begins to glow with a most marvelous light. One of the ministers breaks out singing an ancient chant:

> . . . Rejoice, O earth, in shining splendor,
> radiant in the brightness of your King!
> The Messiah has conquered!
> Glory fills you!
> Darkness vanishes for ever! . . .

The Vigil of Vigils has begun.

In the "Light of Christ," we watch, and wait, and pray, and sing, as, text after text, we relive the whole spiritual journey which brings our community to this night:

> In the beginning
> God created the heavens and the earth . . .

And God said, "Let there be light . . .
(Genesis 1 R.S.V.)

As they walked along together,
Isaac spoke up, "Father!"
He answered, "Yes, my son?"
Isaac asked, "I see that you have the coals and the wood,
but where is the lamb for the sacrifice?"
Abraham answered, "God himself will provide one."
And the two of them walked on together . . .
(Genesis 22)

. . . Moses held out his hand over the sea,
and the Lord drove the sea
back with a strong east wind.
It blew all night
and turned the sea into dry land.
The water was divided,
and the Israelites went through the sea
on dry ground,
with walls of water on both sides . . .
(Exodus 14)

. . . I will use you to show the nations that I am holy.
I will take you from every nation and country
and bring you back to your own land.
I will sprinkle clean water on you
and make you clean from all your idols
and everything else that has defiled you.
I will give you a new heart and a new mind.
I will take away your stubborn heart of stone
and give you an obedient heart.
I will put my spirit in you
and will see to it that you follow my laws
and keep all the commands I have given you.
Then you will live in the land I gave your ancestors.
You will be my people,
and I will be your God . . . "
(Ezekiel 36)

. . . For surely you know that
when we were baptized
into union with Christ Jesus,
we were baptized into union
with his death.
By our baptism, then,
we were buried with him
and shared his death,
in order that,
just as Christ was raised from death
by the glorious power of the Father,
so also we might live a new life . . .
                    (Romans 6)

It has been forty days, now, since any of us has said *"Alleluia."*
It is a word which drops out of our prayer during the desert days of
Lent. But now, as we stand waiting to hear the Good News of what
happened to Jesus in the middle of this night, a solitary cantor begins
to sing:

All the priests take up the song; then the choir; then the whole community, until our Passover *Alleluia* fills the church. As our *Alleluia*
grows, the lights begin to come on again until the whole church is
aglow. It is as though our midnight singing has brought the dawn.

No matter how dark our nights have been, this is the night
which illumines them all. No matter what enslaves us, this is the
night which sets us free. No matter what threatens us, this is the
night which gives us hope. No matter what divides us, this is the
night which unites us. No matter when we are baptized, this is the
night on which each of us is baptized. For us, this is the messianic
"night of nights." It is the most wondrous night of all. It is the night

on which we are given the courage to celebrate fully the mystery of "letting-be."

3. The Synthesis: "Letting-Be" in Stereo

We have been listening carefully to the experience of "letting-be" on both the personal and the messianic channels. What we have said of "letting-go" in stereo applies equally well to the experience of "letting-be": it is one thing to hear the word "let be" on only one channel; it is something else to hear it on both channels at once; and it is something else, still, to live it out freely, in stereo. To be invited to "let be" in stereo, however, is to be invited to take yet another step in the Art of Passingover. It is a step that has a character all its own.

The Stereo Effect

When we are experiencing the "awkward inbetween" in our own lives and hear the Bible speaking with such passion from the silence, the desert, the Sabbath and the vigil, we sometimes pick up a "stereo effect." It comes from hearing "let be" on both the personal and the more-than-personal channels of experience at the same time. If only for a moment, we get the sense that it is O.K. to be "inbetween." We get the sense that we are in good company in "letting-be." We get the sense that it can even be salutary to let life be. When we get this sense, we are being invited to recognize that our personal lives are much more than personal; we are being invited to allow our own lives to become messianic by willingly "letting-be."

The Stereo Response

To become an artist in Passingover, however, it is not enough just to listen to the invitation to "let be"; we have to accept the invitation and act on it. Of course, we can pretend that we never received the stereo invitation in the first place, or try to disregard it. That is the "monophonic response," which is always open to us. If we choose to accept the stereo invitation to "let be," however, our response itself has to be in stereo, for we are accepting an invitation to do what we cannot do by ourselves. It takes more than personal courage, and more than personal energy, to accept the messianic invitation to "let be" and to live it out.

The invitation to "let be" frequently comes to us as a disappointing surprise. After we have "let go," we tend to think that something new will immediately fill the void in our lives. When we discover that this is not how it works, we are greatly disappointed. We may be able to set our jaw and to bear the awkwardness of the void for a while, but then a certain restlessness, a certain impatience, a certain desire to "get on with it" tends to overcome us: ". . . What do I do now?" The Psalmist expresses this impatience well when he complains:

> How much longer will you forget me, Lord?
> Forever?
> How much longer will you hide yourself from me?
> How much longer must I endure trouble?
> How long will sorrow fill my heart day and night?
> How long will my enemies triumph over me?
> *Psalm 13:1–3*

These words carry the pain, the passion, and the impatience of the Psalmist, as he experiences a particularly awkward inbetween. They also carry the question which is at the heart of the messianic experience of "letting-be": How long? How long? How long? *How long?*

There are two answers which the messianic experience of "letting-be" regularly gives to this question—neither of which is particularly consoling.

The first answer to "How long?" is: "None of your business. God alone knows. Your business is to let life be." The last recorded words of the disciples to Jesus are, "Lord, will you at this time restore the kingdom back to Israel?" Jesus' characteristic reply is, "It is not for you to know. . . . " (Acts 1:6–7).

The second answer to "How long?" is: "Just a little longer than you can bear." As cruel as it may seem, this reply is a very revealing one. If our personal lives are to be stretched until they become more than personal—if they are to be stretched until they become messianic—then it is very important that they be stretched beyond what we can do on our own. It is very important that the "letting-be" last just a little longer than we can bear. When we find that we are still "letting-be," even though we can no longer bear it, then we know for sure that we are not doing it alone. Then we know that we are "letting-be" in stereo, through a courage and an energy which are being entrusted to us.

As the experience of "letting-be" starts to go beyond our personal capacity and endurance, an inner gracefulness and an inner peacefulness begin to replace our initial awkwardness. The Psalmist seems to be speaking from this place when he writes:

> Lord, I have given up my pride
>   and turned away from my arrogance.
> I am not concerned with great matters
>   or with subjects too difficult for me.
>
> Instead, I am content and at peace.
> As a child lies quietly in its mother's arms,
>   so my heart is quiet within me.
>
> Israel, trust in the Lord
>   now and forever.
>   *Psalm 131*

This little prayer reflects the innermost character of the stereo response to "letting-be." The Psalmist is at peace, now, waiting on the Lord, just as little Mordechai rested on the Great Rabbi's chest.

Believing as the Messianic Courage
To "Let Be" in Hope

Believing can mean many different things to us, at different times in our lives. At the time when we are experiencing "the awkward inbetween" in our lives, to believe means to have the messianic courage to trust a Power beyond our own and to "let be," in the hope that something creative will come of it. It is to have the courage to listen even more intently to life, from the middle of the desert darkness, and to hope against hope.

Once again, two Hebrew words reflect what it means to believe in a messianic way. When we are being called to "let be," however, they too take on a somewhat different meaning.

First of all, to believe is to say *"Amen"*; it is to say "so be it" to everything that the awkwardness, the desert, the darkness and the silence reveals. It is to say "let it be" to the messianic heartbeat as it resonates within our own lives.

To say *"Amen"* again and again, to "let be," is to utter, and to live, a most creative word. It is to allow ourselves to become rooted in all that actually *is*. It is to allow ourselves to become grounded in the nature of things, and in the Ground of all Being. It is to allow ourselves to become channels of a creative energy far greater than our own. It is to allow the creative "let be" litany of Genesis to see a new day in our own lives. We find ourselves letting our hopes be, and then beginning to be amazed at what they start to become. There is a great realism in this kind of *"Amen"*; it is a most creative word.

When our *"Amen"* to "let be" is firmly established, our act of believing gives birth to a second word: *"Alleluia." "Alleluia"* is a word of praise and joy which begins to well up in us as we experience how creative our *"Amen"* actually is. It wells up in us as we begin to experience ourselves as capable not only of listening in stereo, but of living in stereo as well; we begin to realize that our own lives are capable of carrying and transmitting messianic energy! This discovery brings with it a great joy and a heartfelt hope which let us "praise God" even from the middle of the "awkward inbetween."

As a rule, the *"Alleluia"* side of believing does not come right away. It takes its time. It may take forty days to arrive, as it does in the Vigil of Vigils, or much, much longer, as it frequently does in life. When we first go to the hiding place, we may have a sense of relief which comes from "letting-go" of other things, but it is not long before our relief turns into confusion, fear, boredom, loneliness, and, finally, "cabin fever." If we remain faithful to "letting-be," however, the "cabin fever" frequently turns into "hut happiness." It is as though the awkward pause of "letting-be" becomes pregnant with promise: the silence speaks, the desert blooms, the Sabbath unveils a work to be done, and the vigil reveals an inner light. Then, with many who have gone before us, we begin, not merely enduring, but actually celebrating, the inner gracefulness of "the awkward inbetween"; we join the whole messianic tradition in praising God from the middle of the desert. *"Alleluia"* is a very creative word; it is the "eureka" of believing which resonates, in a very special way, from the middle of the experience of "letting-be."

In this chapter we have been reflecting on "letting-be," both as a personal and as a messianic experience of the "awkward inbetween," and on the stereo response of believing, as the way in which our personal experience becomes messianic. This act of willingly and hope-fully "letting-be" is the second key action in the Art of Passingover. It is the second great step by which we take an active part in the Eighth Day of Creation. As the experience of "letting-be" begins to reveal its promise, we start hearing another word coming from the center of our lives: "Let grow." We can now turn our attention to the third key step in the Art of Passingover, the experience of "letting-grow."

Chapter 5

Letting-Grow
The Experience of Awesome Beginnings

. . . he who is mighty
has done great things for me,
and holy is his name.
Luke 1:49 (R.S.V.)

We may spend a long time, watching and waiting in the silent darkness of "letting-be" before we begin to see the light. We may spend a long time in a deeply personal sort of desert, experiencing what seems to be nothingness, before we begin to experience something new coming from the nothingness. If we have the courage to continue watching, waiting, and "letting-be" in hope, however, new experiences can begin to stir within us. Things may not have changed much on the surface of our lives, but things begin to change considerably in the depths of our lives. We experience new hopes, new possibilities, and new energies beginning to stir within us. It is as though we begin to come alive again, but from the in-side out. From the middle of these inner stirrings, we begin to hear, quite distinctly, a whole new creative word: "Let grow." This word invites us to take still another step in participating in the Eighth Day of Creation. It marks a whole new phase in the Art of Passingover, a phase in which we learn how to work creatively with experiences of heartfelt, wonder-filled, awesome beginnings.

In order to get some sense of what the stereo response to the creative word "let grow" involves, let us listen to it, first of all, on the channel of personal experience, and then on the channel of more-than-personal, messianic experience.

1. Channel One: The Personal Experience of "Letting-Grow" The Gift of "Awesome Beginnings"

The experience of "awesome beginnings" can come to us in many different forms. It can come in the form of an idea for a new project; an insight into how to solve what had seemed to be an insoluble problem; an inspiration for a work of art; a fresh perspective on a troublesome situation; a fond hope that a personal relationship may deepen; an inner prompting to do something different with our lives; an image or vision of what the future could hold; a resolution to change in some way or other; a new value or set of beliefs; a dream of what we might do or become. The experience of "awesome beginnings" can come to us in many different forms.

In whatever form it does come to us, however, the experience of "awesome beginnings" comes as a gift. It comes as a gift which surprises us, enthralls us, excites us, delights us, energizes us, and makes us wonder. It seems to come to us "from nowhere" or "out of the blue"; it is clearly not our doing.

The man who comes out of the hospital with a different approach to life; the mother of four who, after some serious soul-searching, decides to go back to finish her degree; the college freshman who, after an awkward adjustment, begins to feel at home and to find her major field of study; the young rebel who discovers a cause worth working for; the lonely man who finds someone with whom to share his life; the adolescent who begins to experience himself as an adult; the artist who conceives a new work; the agnostic who begins to believe; the alcoholic who starts to build a new life; the middle-aged person who sets out on a second career; the bored retiree who discovers a new way to employ her talents—all of these persons are experiencing the gift of "awesome beginnings."

Giving Birth to a New Work

From the few examples we have cited we can notice that, while the experience of "awesome beginnings" is rooted in a heartfelt inner experience, it is focused on a work which still has to be done. The Germans have a saying which describes this well; they say, "Die Gabe zur Aufgabe wird," that is, "The gift becomes a work." It is one thing to be given a bouquet of roses; it is something else to be given a talent or an inspiration.

From my days as a graduate student, I can remember a dramatic instance of just how "the gift becomes a work." One of my friends in the doctoral program was the envy of us all. While most of us had to spend a year or two trying to find a topic for our research, he entered the program with his topic already in mind: "Confirmation in Catholic Theology in the Past Twenty-Five Years." This was a very clearly defined topic; there were only several books and twenty-some articles written on the subject, and he had most of them on his desk. He set about his work, determined to finish the program in less than three years—a feat unheard of, at that university.

My friend had been working on his dissertation for about six months when a student from Rome visited us. The visitor was shocked when he heard the topic of my friend's thesis; he had just assisted at the defense of a dissertation in Rome on the very same subject!

The visitor's shock was nothing compared to how upset my friend was. He had just lost six months of hard work, together with the prospect of finishing his dissertation in record time. He was understandably upset, angry, frustrated, depressed, and very anxious.

A well-meaning stranger might have tried to console my friend by saying, "Don't worry. It's only a dissertation. It's not your whole life." The problem with that is that, for a graduate student at that stage of the work, the dissertation *is* his whole life!

"What are you going to do now?" I asked him.

"I'm going to make a retreat," he shrugged. "That's what I always do when I'm in trouble."

Several days later he was back on the scene looking more buoyant than ever.

"Have you decided what to do about the dissertation?" I asked.

"No problem," he replied. "Confirmation in *Anglican* Theology in the Past Twenty-Five Years!"

What happened on that retreat? We were not with him, but we can almost see my friend spending the first few days joining the Psalmist in cursing, complaining, and exploring a thousand different ways of saying, "Why me?" Then we can see him facing some of the anxieties and fears that this situation raised within him: "How can I go back to teaching college without a degree?"; "At my age, this is the last chance for me"; "What will my friends think if I fail again?"; "If they give me one of those heavy research topics, I'll never get out of here," et cetera, et cetera. By this time he was probably quite exhausted and beginning to quiet down; he had probably "let go" of his first, anxious reactions, and may even have "let go" of the dissertation itself. He probably found himself much more peaceful now, and more inclined to savor the silence of the retreat, and to let the situation with the dissertation be. Then, up from the silence, came the gift: "The Anglicans! Of course! Why didn't *I* think of that!" Suddenly, he was excited, enthusiastic and filled with energy again.

It is one thing to be given the gift, however, and it is something else to do the work that the gift requires. It is one thing to be given the inspiration; it is something else to see it through to fulfillment. The gift of a new topic gave my friend the vision and the energy for the work he had to do, but it did not do the work for him. He still would have to work hard for a couple of years in order to turn that gift into an acceptable manuscript. It was as my friend dedicated himself to that creative task that "the gift became the work."

As it turned out, the Anglicans had written even less on the topic of Confirmation in the past twenty-five years than the Catholics had, and—what was even more fortunate—it was all in English! My friend finished his dissertation in less than three years, just as he had predicted.

It is hard to exaggerate the importance of the relationship we have been describing between the creative inspiration and the creative work; they are the two sides of the coin of living creatively. If we fail to recognize this, we act as though being creative were merely a matter of being gifted with an unending succession of creative inspirations, visions or dreams. Martin Luther King may have had many inspiring dreams, but the one that made the difference was the one of a racially integrated society; that dream moved him so deeply that he felt obliged to make it public and to dedicate his life to realizing it. Gandhi may have had many inspiring visions, but the one that made the difference was the one of a free and united Mother India; that dream became his lifework.

Dreams and visions of this kind are much more than merely "good ideas" or "wishful thinking"; they are the "awesome beginnings," the seedlings, of a life of creative dedication. They not only point the way toward a creative work, they also give us the inner energy and the personal commitment for doing it. As with any seedling, however, dreams and visions of this kind are very delicate, at first. We have to learn how to take care of them, nurture them, and work with them if they are ever to see the light of day, become mature, and bear their fruit for us and others to enjoy.

If we divorce the creative inspiration from the creative work, however, we tend to become "bright idea" persons. We often are very quick to tell others what they have to do to solve a problem or complete a project. More often than not, what we mean by that is that we have no intention of getting involved in the work itself. The more we divorce the creative inspiration from the creative work, the less we realize how much work and how much time are involved in actually doing what we are thinking about, and the more unreal our inspirations become. The creative inspiration may be so clear in our mind that we feel as though the creative work is practically finished already. It is not finished, however; it is just being conceived. It is in the stage of "awesome beginnings" and may still have a very long way to go before it is fully embodied in a creative work. The creative experience of "letting-grow" is not only a matter of conceiving something new; it is also a matter of giving it birth and bringing it to fruition.

Carrying New Life

I remember being delighted, as a young seminarian, to learn that one of my sisters was pregnant and was expecting a child around Christmastime. I wrote her a letter in which I described how wonderful it must be to be carrying new life during the season of Advent, when Mary herself was pregnant with the Word, and our whole community of faith feels pregnant with the Messiah.

In her reply to me, my sister wrote, "Thanks a lot for your beautiful thoughts, Fran, because, at times, the weight of being pregnant is overwhelming."

I know that her thanks was sincere, but my immediate reaction was total embarrassment; here I was spinning off pious reflections, while she was bearing the burden of carrying new life.

It is not by chance that our minds turn to thoughts of carrying new life when we speak of the experience of "awesome beginnings"; the experience of carrying new life is a primary model for every experience of "letting-grow." When we are hearing the word "let grow" in our lives, it is striking how naturally we fall into using "birthing images" to describe what is going on within us. We speak of how "the seed was planted" in us, or of how "the idea was conceived." We also speak of something "kicking around in us" or of a project being in its "gestation period." We speak of an inspiration as being "pregnant with possibilities," or of a work being "in its sixth month." We speak of our being entrusted with something that "wants to see the light of day," or of a creative work "being aborted" by an adverse set of circumstances. We also speak of experiencing "labor pains," of bringing a project "to term," and of "giving birth" to it. We even speak of ourselves as "being in the womb again," or "being reborn," or "being given a new lease on life," or "living a new life." As we live with this sense of bearing new life, we may find ourselves, as a mother would, adopting a certain regimen or discipline, in order to do so with integrity.

When we use them to express what is going on within our lives, these "images of birthing" are not just fanciful images; they are very powerful reflections of what is actually involved in the experience of "letting-grow." They reflect, in a symbolic way, how the gift of "awesome beginnings" is becoming a work, and sometimes even a life-work, for us. While these "images of birthing" reflect an experience which, physically, is unique to women, they express an experience which, personally, is common to everyone who is being invited to let something creative grow in their lives.

The Fear of "Letting Grow"

If we have been waiting all along for an experience in the Art of Passingover which is problem free, we are destined to be sadly disappointed by the experience of "letting-grow." It is true that, at first, the experience of "awesome beginnings" is frequently one of pure euphoria. It makes us feel excited, optimistic, and energetic again. It is not long, however, before the initial enthusiasm wears off, and we begin to realize how much risk, how much work, and how much energy will have to go into letting whatever we are experiencing within us grow. It is then that we begin feeling the fears and counting the costs that are part of letting something new grow in our lives.

While the promise of something new can delight us, the prospect of it can frighten us as well. It can mean that things will change, persons will change, and we will change. For many of us, changes of that sort are frightening. We are more secure with things as they "always have been."

Nor is that all. At the outset, we do not really know what form our inspiration will finally take as we begin to work with it; that can frighten us as well. A couple may feel called to raise a family, but they come to know what form that family will actually take only as their work together unfolds. In addition, as their common work unfolds, it begins taking on a life of its own, so that, while they continue to be actively involved in letting their family grow, they are no longer fully in control of how it grows. Even if we have a powerful dream, many of us are frightened to undertake something which we will not be able fully to control.

In addition, many of us get frightened by the work of "letting-grow" when we begin to see what demands it will make on our time and energy. We realize that we will have to take personal responsibility for our inspiration and become actively committed to letting it unfold creatively. For many of us, this kind of commitment is a red flag that threatens our personal freedom and frightens us away.

There is always the fear of failure, too. At one level, we may be afraid to begin something that we may not be able to complete. We can almost feel others laughing at us. On another level, we may become afraid that we will never be able to bridge the gap between the inner reality of our inspiration and the outer reality of its creative embodiment. In either case, we are afraid of failing.

By letting something new grow in our lives, we also run the risk of being misunderstood or rejected by others. The growth of something new means that we will be acting, working, or living in a different way and, perhaps, producing something others have never seen before. We have no way of knowing how that will be received by others. "Letting-grow" means running the risk of being misunderstood or rejected, and that can frighten us as well.

It may be less a question of fear than of discouragement, but, sometimes, we can be frightened away from "letting-grow" by the scope of the task or the length of time involved in completing it. If we expect that our inspiration will be realized almost immediately, we may be discouraged as we discover how long it actually takes to move from the wonderful gift of inspiration to the creative realization of it. We may also discover that the creative work that we are called to do is such that we may never see its fruits in our lifetime. We have to have a special courage to be creatively involved in works of this scope.

The Flight from "Letting-Grow"

Although most of us are not inclined to flee from the experience of "awesome beginnings," the fear of the full implications of the experience of "letting-grow" can send us into flight. Two of the most common ways in which we flee from "letting-grow" are by running away either from the outer work or from the inner gift.

On the one hand, we flee from the reality of "letting-grow" by trying to multiply our dreams, rather than by working toward their creative embodiment. In this case, we run away from the work involved in "letting-grow." Rather than commit ourselves to the creative task of allowing the inner gift to become an outer work, we try to repeat the euphoria of the experience of "awesome beginnings." In this way, we begin building a "dream world" which, in time, can become increasingly divorced from the reality of the world outside us.

Another way in which we flee from the reality of "letting-grow" is by giving up the inspiration; we pretend that we never experienced it and go back to "business as usual." "It was only a dream," we say, and we get involved in something "more realistic."

The Courage To "Let Grow"

It takes courage to face the fears, and to avoid the flight patterns which are associated with the experience of "letting-grow." It takes courage to experience the gift of "awesome beginnings" and to explore the ways in which that gift wants to grow and to find creative expression in the world. It takes courage to see a heartfelt hope through its many ups and downs until it "comes of age." It takes courage, and patience, to honor the timing that the integrity of the gift's growth requires: to "let it go," at times; to "let it be," at other times; and to "let it grow," throughout. It takes courage to call on others and on more-than-personal resources for help.

A disciple called out to his teacher of Zen, "Master! I am enlightened! What do I do now?"

"Fetch some wood, and mop the floor," the Master replied.

With the experience of "awesome beginnings," of inner enlightenment, the disciple thinks he has reached the end of the whole discipline of Zen.

The Master's reply suggests that the gift of enlightenment is not an end in itself; it is the beginning of a life dedicated to doing simple tasks with singular inner attentiveness, so that the world may be transformed.

This story of the importance of living and working with the gift has a parallel in the life of Buddha himself. After he experienced his enlightenment, he is said to have been gripped by a great fear. He was afraid that if he tried to express what happened to him, no one would understand; he was then tempted to withdraw totally from society. This is "the last temptation" of Buddha. He overcame that temptation, however, and began to teach. "Someone will understand," he said.

We have been listening to how the creative word "let grow" sounds as it resonates on the channel of personal experience. We have heard how it is an experience of "awesome beginnings" which can take many different forms in many different lives. We also have an intimation of how much courage and work it takes to remain faithful to the experience of "letting-grow" in our lives. In light of that we can turn now to listen to the experience of "letting-grow" on the more-than-personal, messianic channel.

2. Channel Two: The Messianic Experience of "Letting-Grow"

From Genesis to the Apocalypse, the creative word "let grow" knits together the whole biblical tradition. In order to hear it, however, we have to learn to listen, not only to words, but also to the lives of those who live with a sense of mission. When we approach the Bible in this way, it is not long before we find ourselves listening to the lives of the prophets and of the wonder-filled women who people it, for they are people with a purpose; and their purpose is to let the gift which God has given them grow. Let us listen to these lives first of all, and then to the life of a messianic community as it celebrates the experience of "awesome beginnings" in the Easter Vigil.

Listening to the Lives of Prophets

When we listen to the lives of the prophets, what we hear, above all, is a highly personal embodiment of a God-given vocation, or call. In the prophet's original experience of being inspired, this call comes as a gift; as it unfolds in the prophet's on-going mission to his people, this gift becomes a lifework. The prophet is a *nabi*, a "spokesperson" for God, not only in the sense of being called to listen to the Word of God and *proclaim* it, but also in the sense of being called to *embody* it. Each prophet embodies the Word in a uniquely personal way. As he does so, his life becomes a living parable; it becomes a living word, and a personal symbol of the messianic vocation of the community as a whole.

The prophetic experience of "awesome beginnings" starts with the experience of a personal call, or vocation. As the first of the prophets, Moses is a perfect example of how the prophet experiences his call (Exodus 2:11–4:31).

Moses is in exile, leading his father-in-law's sheep across the desert when he comes upon the mountain of God, and is fascinated by a bush that keeps on burning. As Moses draws closer to see what is going on, the Lord speaks to him from the burning bush, " . . . Now I am sending you to the King of Egypt so that you can lead my people out of his country" (Exodus 3:10).

Very characteristically, Moses comes up with a better idea: "No, Lord, please send someone else" (4:13). As he tries to talk God into changing his mind, Moses reveals his own deepest fears and insecurities in face of this awesome commission to "let grow":

> "I am nobody. How can I go to the king and bring the Israelites out of Egypt?"
>
> God answered, "I will be with you, and when you bring the people out of Egypt, you will worship me on this mountain. That will be the proof that I have sent you."
>
> But Moses replied, "When I go to the Israelites and say to them, 'The God of your ancestors sent me to you,' they will ask me, 'What is his name?' So what can I tell them?"
>
> God said, "I am who I am. You must tell them: 'The one who is called I AM has sent me to you.' "
>
> Then Moses answered the Lord, "But suppose the Israelites do not believe me and will not listen to what I say . . . "
>
> (The Lord gives Moses three signs of his God-given mission: the staff-serpent, the healed hand, and the water-blood.)
>
> But Moses said, "No, Lord, don't send me. I have never been a good speaker, and I haven't become one since you began to speak to me. I am a poor speaker, slow and hesitant."
>
> The Lord said to him, "Who gives man his mouth? Who makes him deaf or dumb? Who gives him sight or makes him blind? It is I, the Lord. Now, go! I will help you to speak, and I will tell you what to say."

By this time, it is clear to Moses that the Lord is serious about all of this. It is also clear to him that, as the one chosen to take the lead in Passingover, he will not be relying on his own power. The Lord will be with him every step of the way. With that, Moses returns to Egypt.

Most of the other prophets witness to a similar experience of "awesome beginnings": to a mysterious encounter with God; to a host of personal misgivings about what God proposes; and to the conviction that their mission will be accomplished by the power of God at work in them, regardless of how overwhelming the odds against them may be.

When their people are experiencing hard times, the prophets begin to prophesy from their experience of "awesome beginnings." They stop threatening the people with the "painful endings" which were meant to bring them to repentance, and begin encouraging them to rejoice and renew their lives through the gifts the Lord is about to shower on them. Isaiah's oracles of Emmanuel, "God-with-us" (6–12), the "Book of the Consolation" (Isaiah 40–55); Jeremiah's prophecies of the homecoming of the exiles, the new covenant, and the restoration of the Jerusalem (30–33); and Ezekiel's visions of the renewal of the land, the people, the Temple, and Israel (36–37; 40–48), are all proclamations of "awesome beginnings" to a troubled people, and prophetic invitations to take heart, and to "let grow."

As we listen to the lives of the prophets, we realize that the recurrent cartoons in which we see a prophet carrying a sign which reads, "REPENT," tell only half the story of the prophetic vocation. The other side of the sign reads, "REJOICE AND RENEW." These are the "three R's" of the prophetic vocation; they correspond directly to the three creative words of the Art of Passingover: "let go"; "let be"; "let grow."

Listening to the Lives of Wonder-filled Women

The prophets are not the only ones in the Bible whose lives embody the word "let grow"; the prophetic lives of many wonder-filled biblical women embody it, as well. For example, let us listen to the description of Mary's call to be the mother of Jesus:

> The angel came to her and said, "Peace be with you! The Lord is with you and has greatly blessed you!"
>
> Mary was deeply troubled by the angel's message, and she wondered what his words meant. The angel said to her, "Don't be afraid, Mary; God has been gracious to you. You will become pregnant and give birth to a son, and you will name him Jesus. He will be great and will be called the Son of the Most High God. The Lord God will make him a king, as his ancestor David was, and he will be the king of the descendants of Jacob forever; his kingdom will never end!"
>
> Mary said to the angel, "I am a virgin. How, then, can this be?"
>
> The angel answered, "The Holy Spirit will come on you, and God's power will rest upon you. For this reason the holy child will be called the Son of God. Remember your relative Elizabeth. It is said that she cannot have children, but she herself is now six months pregnant, even though she is very old. For there is nothing that God cannot do."
>
> "I am the Lord's servant," said Mary; "may it happen to me as you have said."
>
> *Luke 1:28–38*

Mary has misgivings as she hears this awesome invitation to "let grow" just as Moses did. Once it becomes clear that it will be God's own doing, however, Mary agrees to become wonderfully pregnant with the Word of God through her "let it be"—her *"fiat."* She consents to embody God's gift, to carry it within her, and to let it grow.

It is not long before Mary is pictured as breaking into song. In her *"Magnificat"* she sings an ecstatic song from the middle of the experience of "awesome beginnings." In it, Mary develops a theme which resonates throughout the history of Israel: she celebrates God's loving kindness for those who have been brought low, and relates her personal experience to the whole history of the Promise:

"My heart praises the Lord;
        my soul is glad because of God my Savior,
        for he has remembered me, his lowly servant!
From now on all people will call me happy,
        because of the great things
        the Mighty God has done for me.
His name is holy;
        from one generation to another
        he shows mercy to those who honor him.
He has stretched out his mighty arm
        and scattered the proud with all their plans.
He has brought down mighty kings from their thrones,
        and lifted up the lowly.
He has filled the hungry with good things,
        and sent the rich away with empty hand.
He has kept the promise he made to our ancestors,
        and has come to the help of his servant Israel.
He has remembered to show mercy to Abraham
        and to all his descendants forever!"
                                        Luke 1:46–55

Mary's experience of "awesome beginnings" is one of being filled and "lifted up" by the Lord. As Matthew comments on Mary's experience of her calling, he sees it to fulfill the ancient prophecy of Isaiah 7:14 concerning the birth of the messianic king:

Now all this happened in order to make come true what the Lord had said through the prophet, "A virgin will become pregnant and have a son, and he will be called Immanuel" (which means, "God is with us").
                                        Matthew 1:22–23

By carrying the Messiah within her, Mary is seen to be a prototype and a symbol of what the entire messianic community is called to be. She is a woman "after God's own heart." As the Catholic community honors Mary in this way, it sees her experience to be fore-shadowed, not only in the prophecy of Isaiah, but also in the primordial prophecy—the "protogospel"—which follows the Fall:

> Then the Lord God said to the snake, "You will be pun-ished for this. . . . I will make you and the woman hate each other; her offspring and yours will always be enemies. Her offspring will crush your head, and you will bite their heel."
>
> *Genesis 3:14–15*

Mary is but one of the many wonder-filled women in the Bible who are called to embody the creative word, "let grow." She is joined by a whole company of apparently "useless" women who, like the desert itself, are thought to be incapable of ever bearing new life. At first these noble women are often embarrassed and deeply troubled by their barrenness. They experience it as a reproach, but as they "let it be" in hope, their barrenness becomes the fertile soil in which God has his way. It is from their "nothingness" that some most cre-ative stirrings begin to come.

When Sarah is told that she will bear the Son of the Promise in her old age, she laughs. But God has the last laugh. A year later, Sarah begets a son and calls him Isaac, that is, "God smiles." Real-izing that the joke has been on her, she invites everyone else to laugh along (Genesis 18:1–15; 21:1–8). In a similar way, the barren womb of Hanna bears Samuel, the prophet who will anoint David king (I Samuel 1); and the sterile womb of Elizabeth becomes the first des-ert in which the Baptizer is nourished, and from which he emerges (Luke 1).

Sarah, Hanna, Elizabeth, Mary—these are but a few of the won-der-filled biblical women who embody the creative word "let grow" by celebrating experience of "awesome beginnings" with their lives. Through their fidelity to their personal call, the life of each of these women is a symbol of what the whole messianic community is called to be; a "wonder-filled woman," gloriously pregnant with the Word, who lovingly lets it grow.

> Jerusalem, you have been like a childless woman,
> but now you can sing and shout for joy.

Now you will have more children
than a woman whose husband never left her.

                                        Isaiah 54:1

Celebrating "Awesome Beginnings"

The lives of the prophets and of the wonder-filled biblical women are not the only lives which carry the creative word "let grow"; the life of a celebrating messianic community carries it, as well. As the community to which I belong celebrates the experience of "awesome beginnings" in the Great Vigil, we can hear the word "let grow" resonating, above all, in the symbols of the Word, the Water, the Bread, and the Cross.

The Symbol of the Word

As the vigil continues, the community welcomes the Word by singing the Easter *Alleluia*. Then we stand and listen attentively as, in the middle of this most wondrous night, the celebrant proclaims the Good News:

> Very early on Sunday morning the women went to the tomb, carrying the spices they had prepared. They found the stone rolled away from the entrance to the tomb, so they went in; but they did not find the body of the Lord Jesus. They stood there puzzled about this, when suddenly two men in bright shining clothes stood by them. Full of fear, the women bowed down to the ground, as the men said to them, "Why are you looking among the dead for one who is alive? He is not here; he has been raised. Remember what he said to you while he was in Galilee: 'The Son of Man must be handed over to sinful men, be crucified, and three days later rise to life.'"
>
> Then the women remembered his words, returned from the tomb, and told all these things to the eleven disciples and all the rest. The women were Mary Magdalene, Joanna, and Mary the mother of James; they and the other

women with them told these things to the apostles. But the apostles thought that what the women said was nonsense, and they did not believe them. But Peter got up and ran to the tomb; he bent down and saw the grave cloths but nothing else. Then he went back home amazed at what had happened.

Luke 24:1–12

We break out singing our *Alleluia* all over again, to celebrate this most "awesome beginning."

It is almost midnight, now; but for us, this Word marks the dawning of the New Day. It is as though the tomb at which we have been waiting for so long has become a womb, and the whole community has become wondrously pregnant with new life.

The Symbol of the Water

As a response to the Good News, we bless the water for baptism. We usually think of water as coming from a faucet, or a well, if we think of its origin at all. But tonight we are much more mindful of the origin of things. We know that the water which we bless this night has come a long, long way to our baptismal font. This water was hovered over by the Spirit at the dawn of creation; it flooded the world in the time of Noah, to clear the way for a new creation; it stood at attention as the Israelites passed through the Red Sea unharmed; it flowed in the Jordan when Jesus was baptized; it flowed again from Jesus' side as he died on the cross; and it flows again tonight, into our baptismal font. This water has come a long, long way to our baptismal font. We welcome it, by immersing the Passover Candle into it, and praying:

We ask you Father, with your Son
    to send the Holy Spirit upon the waters of this font.
May all who are buried with Christ
    in the death of baptism
    rise also with him to newness of life.

Water is an awesome, paradoxical reality. It can deal death, as it does in storms, and floods, and drownings; it can also cleanse and bring new life and growth, as it does day after day in our lives. Perhaps that is why the symbol of water speaks to us so loudly in the middle of this night in which we celebrate the paradox of life coming from death.

Since we have already been baptized as children, we only renew our baptismal vows now, and wince and snicker as the celebrant sprinkles us all with the water.

Our renewal of our baptismal vows is a rather restrained celebration of the symbol of water; we want to experience its meaning without getting too wet, without mussing our hair, or wrinkling our clothes; but we realize that we have known much less restrained celebrations, in the past. In fact . . . we can almost see ourselves . . . on this very night . . . in the early days of our community . . .

We stand together in the vestibule of a building built especially for Passingover. The celebrant tells us unceremoniously, "Take off your clothes." So we strip and stand there naked and trembling, as we promise to turn from darkness, and to spend all of our days living in the light of Christ. Then we are led into a very special room: it is the womb of the community. Its ceiling and walls are covered with mosaics of saints who seem to be smiling and dancing in the light of our flickering torches. In the middle of the room is a large pool of water. One by one, we are led down into the waters of the pool. Then, the bishop asks us if we really believe each of the three tenets of the Creed which the community holds sacred. Each time we say, "I do believe," the deacon almost drowns us in the pool. Three times he pulls us up again, just in the nick of time. As we gasp for breath, the assistant ministers lead us up from the pool, lovingly anoint us with fragrant oil, and wrap us in a new white robe.

When all of us are ready, we process into the church where the community is keeping vigil. The community greets us with loud cries of, "The Messiah is risen! The Messiah is risen!" We are the fruit of this long vigil—the "newly born"—and the community's cause for great rejoicing. As the community continues to welcome us with shouts, and cries, and warm embraces, we are over-whelmed with a sense of belonging, and overjoyed by this extraordinary experience of "awesome beginnings."

By comparison with this ancient celebration, the renewal of our baptismal promises is a rather restrained celebration of the symbol of water. But maybe not. Who knows what some of us have lived through during this past year? We were all baptized as children by a priest, it is true, but perhaps some of us were baptized again by life itself this year. As we stand together this night, we have no way of knowing how close to death some of us may have come during this past year, or how wondrously we may have been raised up to new life. Perhaps this somewhat sedate sprinkling of water means more to some of us than we can ever say. Perhaps it is a deeply personal experience of "awesome beginnings." We have no way of knowing.

The Symbol of the Bread

It has been three days now since we have blessed and broken the Bread as Jesus did. As we bring our gifts of bread and wine to the altar again, we realize that we are hungry. We also realize that our bread has come a long, long way to this table. This is the bread which sustained the Israelites in their flight to freedom; it is the bread which nourished Elijah on his journey to the mountain of God; it is the bread which Jesus multiplied to feed his hungry people in the desert; it is the unleavened bread of the Passover; it is the bread which Jesus blessed at his last meal; it is the Body of the Risen Lord; the food for Passingover; the bread of "awesome beginnings"; it is unlike any other bread we have ever known. We eat any other bread so that it may become like us; we eat this bread so that we may be-come like it. We take it, we bless it, we break it, and we share it again, just as Jesus did; it is the unleavened Bread of Passingover:

On the night he was betrayed,
he took bread and gave you thanks and praise.
He broke the bread, gave it to his disciples, and said:

Take this, all of you, and eat it:
this is my body which will be given up for you.

When supper was ended, he took the cup.
Again he gave you thanks and praise,
gave the cup to his disciples, and said:
Take this, all of you, and drink from it:
this is the cup of my blood,
the blood of the new and everlasting covenant.
It will be shed for you and for all,
so that sins may be forgiven.

Do this in memory of me.

In the middle of the night, we break our fast on this very special bread and wine. We eat and drink these gifts of "letting grow" as we celebrate our deepest communion in the Passingover of Jesus and praise our God, from whom all blessings flow.

The Symbol of the Cross

As the first rays of the sun rise over the Abbey on Easter morning, they light up the cross on the hill which itself seems to be dancing now. It is draped with a beautiful long white banner trimmed in orange and gold which glistens in the sun as it waves in the gentle dawn breeze. During the long night of vigil, one of the brothers climbed the cross and draped it in glory. The torch which has burned before it for three days now gives way to the sun. The cross which spoke to us so powerfully of "letting go" on Friday, the cross which spoke to us so intimately of "letting be" on Saturday, now speaks to us triumphantly of "letting grow." As it welcomes the sun this Easter morning, the cross speaks to us of the entire Art of Passingover, and of every step along the way. In this triumphant cross we celebrate the full paradox of life-giving death; the paradox is embraced; the curse becomes a blessing; the threat becomes a promise; and the bane of mankind becomes the banner of our Victorious King. Until Pentecost comes, the cross on the hill will be draped like this, joyously inviting us to "let grow."

3. The Synthesis: "Letting-Grow" in Stereo

There was an Irish parish priest who would hitch up his horse and buggy each week and visit the members of his little church. For the most part, he used to enjoy the ride and the beauty of the countryside—that is, except for the sight of one field. It was deserted, abandoned, full of rocks and brambles, with a broken down old fence. It was so ugly, the priest could hardly stand the sight of it.

Then one day, a young man moved into the area and bought the field. Little by little, he cleared away the brambles and the rocks. He used the rocks to build a sturdy wall and replaced the old, broken fence with a brand new one which he made himself. Then he planted a small garden and began to care for it.

The parish priest was delighted to see how much the field had changed. He actually looked forward to seeing it now as he made his weekly rounds.

One day, as he was passing by, the priest saw the young man out working in the field. He stopped and went over to talk to him.

"Michael," he called out, "may I have a word with you?"

The young man stopped his work and came over to greet the priest.

"Michael," the priest said, "I just want to tell you that this field is a delight to my heart. You and the Lord are doing a fine job with it."

"Thank you kindly, Father," the young man replied. "You should have seen it when God was doing it all by himself!"

The Stereo Effect and Response

In a light-hearted way, this little story highlights for us the central paradox of "letting-grow" in a messianic way: God *and* us, working together.

On the one hand, the gift and the work of "letting-grow" must truly come from a Power beyond our own. This is the side of the paradox which the parish priest is trying to underline for Michael. From this side of the paradox we experience the "let" in "letting-grow" in a primarily passive, or receptive, way. It means we have to get out of the way. The Psalmist is speaking from this side of the paradox, when he writes:

> If the Lord does not build the house,
> > the work of the builders is useless;
> if the Lord does not protect the city,
> > it does no good for the sentries to stand guard.
> It is useless to work so hard for a living,
> > getting up early and going to bed late.
> For the Lord provides for those he loves,
> > while they are asleep.
>
> *Psalm 127:1–2*

On the other hand, the gift, and the work, must truly be our own. This is the side of the paradox that Michael is trying to underline for his parish priest. From this side of the paradox, we experience the "let" in "letting-grow" in a primarily active and creative way. It means that we have to be willing to roll up our sleeves and to take part in letting the creative work unfold. At first, this side of the paradox may bring with it some strong personal misgivings about whether or not we can do it. Such misgivings are not only very common, they are also very important in the experience of "letting-grow"; they remind us that the Art of Passingover is a highly personal work which we cannot do alone.

So, on the one hand, the gift and the work of "awesome beginnings" must truly be beyond us; on the other hand, this gift and this work must truly be our own. It boggles the mind when we cup these two hands and try to listen to them both at the same time, but this is how it feels when we begin to hear the "stereo effect" of the personal invitation to "let grow" in our lives. In whatever form it comes, this invitation takes us back to Genesis:

> So God created human beings, making them to be like himself. He created them male and female, blessed them, and

said, "Have many children, so that your descendants will live all over the earth and bring it under their control. I am putting you in charge of the fish, the birds, and all the wild animals. . . . "

Genesis 1:27–28

This text speaks of God's primordial invitation to us to be partners with him in his most creative work. Merely hearing a stereo invitation or inspiration such as this, however, does not care for the environment, clear away any brambles, move any rocks, build any walls, create any gardens, raise any families, or realize any dreams. In order to do that, we have to have the courage to respond in stereo to the invitation "let grow"; we have to have the messianic courage to believe.

Believing as the Messianic Courage to "Let Grow" in Love

If we were to describe the work of Michael as he reclaimed the abandoned field, we would have to say that it was "a labor of love." If we were to describe the work of the teachers, artists, craftsmen, parents, cooks, gardeners, doctors, ministers, heroes, and friends who have touched our lives most deeply, we would probably have to say that it was "a labor of love" as well. We may find it hard to describe just what is so special about these persons, but we have no difficulty at all noticing the special quality of attentiveness, caring, and dedication which characterizes their work and their lives. They are persons who are clearly engaged in "a labor of love."

A little Hasidic saying describes what it is like, in the beginning, when we get involved in a messianic "labor of love":

When you discover
a new way of serving
the Lord,
carry it around
for nine months,
under your heart.

This little saying goes right to the heart of the messianic experience of "letting-grow." "Letting-grow" is an experience of "won-der-filled beginnings" in which we are animated and energized by a love that is beyond our own. It is an experience of being entrusted with a gift which is beyond our own doing, and of being invited to treasure and nurture that gift in an inward way, as a wonder-filled woman would carry a child, until it is old enough and strong enough to see the light of day. It is an experience of discovering that the love-gift has a life and a timing all its own, and of learning how to let it unfold in its own way. It is an experience of loving something new into being. When we have the messianic courage to "let grow" in this way, believing itself becomes a "labor of love."

We can see from this that, at its deepest level, the experience of "awesome beginnings" is rooted in an experience of being loved into life again by a love beyond anything we can imagine. At first, that love takes the form of an inner gift, but it does not stop there. The gift is the seedling of a work still to be done—of a "new way of serving the Lord"—and that work is to be animated by the very same more-than-personal love which characterizes the gift. When we get personally involved in "a labor of love" like this, we begin to realize that this is what the Art of Passingover is really all about; it is all about the way in which this experience of a more-than-personal love trans-forms our lives and our world by growing from the inside out.

If we are to survive and to grow physically, we need an atmo-sphere in which earth, air, fire and water sustain us; if we are to live and grow creatively, such an atmosphere is not enough. Ultimately, the atmosphere which creative life and growth requires is one of messianic courage, trust, hope, and love. We may not be aware of it at first, but, as we practice the Art of Passingover, we are actively involved in building this messianic environment. When we are "let-ting-go," we are building an atmosphere of trust with a vital Energy beyond our own. When we are "letting-be," we are building an at-mosphere of hope with a creative Power beyond our own. When we are "letting grow," we are building an atmosphere of love with a Be-nevolence beyond our own. This is how the messianic courage of be-lieving unfolds in the Art of Passingover, and, as it does so, this is the kind of environment that such courage creates.

At first, "letting-go" in trust, "letting-be" in hope, and "letting-grow" in love may strike us as very different, and quite unrelated, experiences. As we become more experienced in the Art of Passing-over, however, and find ourselves, once again, actively involved in "a labor of love," we begin to realize that these three actions are intimately related as distinct moments in the one creative movement of Passingover. We begin to recognize these three experiences as the three faces which our believing assumes as it becomes messianic and creatively transforms us and our world.

Although the experience of "awesome beginnings" is at the heart of "letting-grow," there is much more involved in "letting-grow" than that. As the gift becomes a work on both the inside and the outside of our life, it initiates us into an on-going experience of "awesome unfoldings" in which we are increasingly surprised by the wonder-filled ways in which our "labor of love" moves toward its completion. Not only the beginnings but also the unfoldings of a messianic work in us are awe-inspiring; they are an experiment in stereophonic wonder. This experience of the "awesome unfoldings" of a creative work has a character all its own which we will explore in the next section, when we describe how we begin to personify the Art of Passingover through our dedication to living creatively.

The experience of "letting-grow" in love can also be summed up in the two little words which characterize messianic believing at every phase of the Art of Passingover: "*Amen*" and "*Alleluia.*"

After a sometimes prolonged experience of "the awkward in-between" of "letting-be," our first intimation of "awesome beginnings" often brings with it such a spontaneous "*Alleluia!*" that almost eclipses the "*Amen*" which lets it arrive. This "*Alleluia*" marks the other side—the discovery side—of the experience of "letting-be." It often comes as such a release from watching and waiting that it is as though the "*Amen*," the "So be it," and the "*Alleluia*," the "Praise God," of "letting be" become just one ecstatic word as we receive the gift involved in "letting-grow."

As we begin to realize that the gift which we receive in "letting-be" is meant to become a work, however, and to anticipate the difficulties which will be involved in that, our "*Alleluia*" becomes somewhat more muted. Then we hear the invitation to "let grow" in love waiting for our "*Amen.*" Once we express our "*Amen,*" the "*Alleluia*" begins to return to mark our experiences of "awesome unfoldings."

"*Amen*" and "*Alleluia,*" then, are two little words which sum up the messianic courage it takes to believe at every phase of its growth. As a stereo response to the invitation to "let grow" in love, however, these two little words also express the full scope of the Art of Passingover and the way in which we begin to personify it. By the time that we begin to realize that, *"Amen"* and *"Alleluia"* have often become much more than "two little words" for us; they have become twins expressing the full mystery of how messianic creativity unfolds within us. Our *"Amen"* resolutely carries our commitment to living creatively, and our *"Alleluia"* enthusiastically reflects our wonder as we experience God doing his work through us.

It seems like a long time ago that we left our mountain climber in the cloud of "letting-be." We can now see that his long journey has at least one more step to take:

. . . Then the Lord spoke up. "Are you still there?" he asked.

"Yes, Lord," the mountain climber replied, "I am still here. It's strange. Even though I can't see, and I feel as though I am doing nothing, I am at peace in this place now. It is good to be here."

"Listen," the Lord said. "I need your help. Will you help me?"

"Of course I will help you, Lord. What do you want me to do for you?"

"One of my friends is stuck on the mountainside," the Lord replied. "Will you go and help?"

The mountain climber shrugged his shoulders. "Lord," he said, "I'd really like to help you, but you know that I'm not much good at mountain climbing anymore. Besides, I don't even know who or where your friend is, so how can I find the way?"

"Do not worry," the Lord answered. "I will be with you. When you lift your hands to me in prayer, I will raise you up and show you the way."

"But, Lord," the mountain climber objected, "your friend doesn't know me from Adam. What if I'm asked who sent me. What will I say, then?"

The Lord said, "If anyone asks, just say LET BE sent you."

"So be it, Lord," the mountain climber replied, and he stretched out his arms in prayer.

For a while, all was very still. But then the mountain climber felt himself being raised up on a gentle breeze. At first he floated through the cloud; then he broke through into full daylight. Beneath him, he saw a more breathtaking view of the mountains, and the hills, and the rivers, and the earth than he had ever before seen. He soared on the gentle breeze, marveling at the beauty below. Then, far below, he noticed someone stuck on the mountainside. As he drew closer, he saw that it was a woman, hanging onto the branch of a tree. She was unable to climb up, and unable to climb down. All she could do was to hang on for dear life.

Without making a noise, the mountain climber grabbed onto a nearby tree and just hung there.

It wasn't long before the woman noticed him. "Thank God," she cried out. "I thought I was alone, here. Did you hear what the Lord said? Let go! He must think I'm crazy! What's he talking about?"

The woman watched in disbelief as the mountain climber let go and disappeared from her sight.

"Well," she thought to herself, "at least I'll have company."

Then she let go . . .

Part III

PERSONIFYING THE ART OF PASSINGOVER

The Experience of Awesome Unfoldings

Introduction

"All that matters is that one is created anew."

Galatians 6:15
(New American Bible)

We have been describing the Art of Passingover as a personal invitation to living creatively. In Part One, we have seen how we can be tempted to practice the Art by listening so intently to life that we are able to hear the messianic heartbeat at the center of it. In Part Two, we have seen how we can be initiated into the Art by allowing the messianic heartbeat and ours to become one in "letting-go," "letting-be" and "letting-grow." In Part Three, we want to describe how we become artists in the Art of Passingover by Passingover again and again, and to suggest what happens to us, and to our environment, as we do so.

When we first learn how to dance we feel very awkward. We also feel very self-conscious. We are concentrating so hard on getting it right that we cannot think of anything else. In addition, we may be fully involved in counting to ourselves "one, two, and-a-three; one, two, and-a-three." If we happen to be dancing with a partner who would like to talk, that makes it even more awkward. There is no way we can carry on a polite conversation and keep concentrating on keeping our feet, our hands, our body, and our counting all going on at the same time. For us, dancing is so complicated.

Our beginner's awkwardness is in stark contrast to the gracefulness of experienced dancers. They make dancing look simple and easy. They are not at all self-conscious. In fact, they seem to be completely self-forgetful when they dance. They move so gracefully and so naturally that there seems to be no difference between them and the dancing. By the way they dance, and often by the way they walk, they personify the art of dancing.

The contrast between the awkwardness of the beginner and the gracefulness of experience in any art applies, as well, to the Art of Passingover. At first, we are extremely self-conscious and extremely awkward in how we move from "letting-go," through "letting-be," to "letting-grow." We move through these experiences one at a time, with little or no sense of their being parts of a whole cycle of messianic creativity. When we get through them, we give a sigh of relief now that "that's over."

Then we begin to realize that going through one cycle of basic experiences does not make an artist. Artists do not "try their hand" at an art; they dedicate their lives to it. We begin to realize that our experience of Passingover is just the beginning; it is only an invitation. It invites us to dedicate our whole life to living creatively by continually growing messianically in trust, hope, and love so that we, and the world in which we live, may be transformed.

It is at this point that we are sorely tempted to give it all up and try something else, just as many artists are at turning points in their artistic development. To accept the invitation to live creatively means that we are willing to Passover, not once and for all, but again and again. It means that we are willing to practice the Art of Passingover day in and day out. It means that we are willing to learn how to do freely and gracefully what we once did so reluctantly and awkwardly. It means that we are willing to do what is beyond our own doing and our control. It means that we are open to living without knowing the agenda, and to being continually surprised by how the artwork of our life unfolds.

By accepting this invitation and dedicating ourself to living creatively, we begin to personify the Art of Passingover and the Eighth Day of creation begins to be realized through the artwork of our own life. This is an experience of "awesome unfoldings."

To the casual observer of the Art of Passingover, "awesome" might seem a trifle overstated. As we dedicate our life to practicing the Art of Passingover, however, "awesome" does not seem overstated at all; it describes just what the whole experience is like. It is awesome to experience a messianic power, which we cannot explain, creatively at work in our own life. It is awesome to experience the freedom which comes from the "not-having" and "not-doing" of "letting-go." It is awesome to experience new life coming from the "nothingness" of "letting-be." It is awesome to experience how creative the "not-doing" of "letting-grow" actually is. It is awesome to experience the artwork of our life unfolding in ways we could never have imagined. "Surprising?" Yes. "Graceful?" True. "Wonderful?" Indeed. But, basically, "awesome."

In this section, we will be describing what it means to personify the Art of Passingover by highlighting the on-going nature of the Art. The specific way in which we personify the Art of Passingover is unique to the life of each of us, but the general direction in which we move is common to all who practice the Art; we all move in the direction of continually growing toward what is, ultimately, beyond our own doing. In the following chapters, therefore, we will describe the Art of Passingover as a messianic way of growing creatively toward Life, Peace, Freedom, Love, God, and A New Creation.

Chapter 6

Growing Messianically Toward Life

> " . . . I say to you,
> unless a grain of wheat
> falls into the earth
> and dies,
> it remains alone;
> but if it dies,
> it bears much fruit."
> *John 12:24 (R.S.V.)*

In these testamental words, Jesus sums up the whole Art of Passing-over; it is an art wholly dedicated to living more creatively and more fruitfully by living gracefully through the experience of dying.

Living Through the Experience of Dying

As we practice the Art of Passingover, we begin to personify the truth of this saying of Jesus. Again and again, we willingly die by "letting-go" and "letting-be," only to discover the rich harvest that awaits us in "letting-be" and "letting-grow."

To face death with such willingness is revolutionary in this culture. Our culture is largely based on the denial of death in any of its forms. For most of us, death is the opposite of life, so we deny it in order to live in peace. In the Art of Passingover, however, we experience death and life as organically related parts of a larger whole; we experience them as inextricably wedded to one another within the messianic process of growth and creativity. So, rather than deny death, we affirm it by creatively living through it; in order to become what we are not, we willingly die to what we are. That is how it is in the Art of Passingover.

As we begin to experience the on-going interrelatedness of life

134

and death in practice, our whole approach to human growth, and to how life unfolds, changes. Formerly, we may have thought that the cycle of human life begins with physical birth and ends with physical death. Given the bias of our culture, we may even have graded the stages along the way on the basis of how close they came to death. So, we gave youth a decided "plus," middle age a perplexed "plus-minus with a question mark," and old age a definite "minus," if we considered it at all.

With some experience in the Art of Passingover, however, we begin to see that this view of human growth represents much less than half of the story. Our own experience begins to teach us how many deaths we have to die in order to grow toward Life, and how marvelously these experiences of dying mark not merely the end of a life, but the beginning of its creative transformation as well. In light of this experience, we no longer find it adequate to portray the cycle of human growth as a curve which begins with birth and ends with death. We begin to envision it more as a recurrent movement through a messianic cyclotron, through which our life circulates from life to death and death to life, again and again. This way of experiencing the growth of persons does not make the experience of dying again and again any less frightening or painful for us, but it does keep us mindful of the direction in which our growth is moving: " . . . if it dies, it produces much fruit."

As we grow toward life by recurrently living through death, a basic transformation in the quality of our lives also begins to take place. It is as though we begin to live from the other side of death. We not only know what it is to be continually threatened, broken, and chastened by the experience of dying; we also know what it is to be spiritually enlarged and enriched by it. We then begin to live with the intensity, the integrity, the equilibrium, and, above all, the gratitude of persons whose brush with death has lent a more-than-personal sense of purpose and direction to their lives. To begin living in this way is to begin living a qualitatively new life.

It is clear that we are using the word "dying" here in a symbolic sense, but that does not make the experience which we are describing any less real. As we practice the Art of Passingover, we find that the symbolic becomes real. We discover that the messianic life which we are living is carried primarily by symbols which have a reality all of their own. While it is true that the dying we experience in Passingover is sometimes not the same as physical death, it is much more than a mere metaphor. It is a symbolic death which is very real. No one who has ever died in this way has to be told how real it is.

As we continue to grow toward Life through the experience of dying gracefully, we begin to notice another significant change in the quality of our lives. In increasingly diversified and wonder-filled ways, we begin to experience the truth that none of us lives, and none of us dies, alone. We begin to experience, in a deeply personal way, the life and death of each of us, affecting us all; we experience the living and dying of each person, and of every community, as part of a whole messianic ecology in which all of life is mysteriously interwoven. Through this experience we begin to live with a capacity for compassion and a sense of community which is beyond anything we had known before; we begin to live a qualitatively new life.

The Sense of Messianic Timing

As we continue to practice the Art of Passingover, we begin to notice another significant change in how we experience the growth and unfoldment of human lives: our sense of timing begins to change. It begins to move from the outside to the inside of our life.

We are accustomed to tell time by looking at our clocks, our goals, our agendas, and our programs. It is not long before we begin to realize that the Art of Passingover does not move in terms of our clocks, our goals, our agendas, and our programs; it moves at a much deeper level of life. As we learn to move with it, we begin to learn how to tell time, not just with our heads, but with our hearts and with our lives. We learn how to "let go" of our clocks, our goals, our agendas, our programs, and our own willfulness, in order to learn to tell time in a messianic way. In ways we often cannot explain, we begin to know when it is time to "let go" in trust, when it is time to "let be" in hope, and when it is time to "let grow" in love. We begin to develop a messianic sense of timing.

At first, much of our pain and confusion in the Art of Passingover comes from the fact that we do not yet know how to tell time in a messianic way. We are often pushing to "letting-grow" when it is actually time to "let go." We are "letting be" when it is time to "let grow." We are "letting-grow" when it is time to "let be." More often than not, we are either anxiously forcing the timing of our growth toward Life, or sadly lagging behind it. In other words, we are having a hard time telling what time it is in our life.

What time is it in our life, then, when life is inviting us to "let go" in trust? We may wish it were otherwise, but, in an inward way, it is definitely dusk. It is twilight time. The activities of the day are coming to an end. We can feel that. We can still see the outline of all that the daytime has brought, but it is fading into the shadows. It lacks the vitality and the reality it once had. It is getting dark. It is that time of life.

More broadly still, when we are "letting-go," it is fall in our lives. The summer's growth is over. The harvest is in, and some of the fruit is going to seed. The seeds are falling to the ground, taking with them a good part of what our life has meant. It is a melancholy time, the end of a season.

What time is it when life is inviting us to "let be" in hope"? It is clearly nighttime. It is often so dark that we cannot see a thing. It is a time of watching and waiting until our life becomes acclimatized to the night so that it may discover, in the darkness, the possibilities of a new day. It is an anxious time, an awkward time, a quiet time, a most mysterious time.

More broadly, when we are "letting-be," it is wintertime in our life. It is a time for hibernating. On the outside, our life seems to be sterile and unproductive; nothing seems to be going on. On the inside, we may feel as though we are dead and buried, but our life moves imperceptibly toward its roots. It is a time of patient waiting until life begins to stir again from within so that we may know another season.

What time is it when life is inviting us to "let grow" in love? There can be little question that it is dawn. It is the beginning of a new day. What we have experienced in the darkness begins to seek expression in the light. It is also daytime. The gift that we have experienced inwardly is now becoming a work which we are engaged in outwardly as well. It is a joyous time, a season of new growth.

More broadly, when we are "letting-be," it is springtime and summertime in our lives. It is a time of joy, a time of new life, a new season of growth. Our energy is welling upward and outward, once again, to make a creative difference in the world.

In speaking not merely of cosmic timing, but of messianic timing, we are speaking symbolically again. We are speaking not of a timing which reflects where the earth is in its movement around the sun, but of a timing which reflects where persons are in their movement toward living creatively. We are speaking about a deeply personal, highly subjective, and symbolic kind of timing which is, nevertheless, very real. There is no denying the reality and the importance of the sense of timing which allows Albert Camus to write, "In the middle of winter, I discovered within himself an invincible summer." As we practice the Art of Passingover, we begin to speak, and live, in a similar way. We begin to develop an inward sense of messianic timing which lets us know when it is time to "let go" in trust, when it is time to "let be" in hope, and when it is time to "let grow" in love.

As we develop this inner sense of messianic timing, it allows us to experience our lives unfolding in two time frames, simultaneously. At times we experience the coincidence of solar and messianic—of outer and inner—time in our lives. The sun-related rhythm of many traditions of prayer and the season-related character of many religious feasts are meant to foster and to reflect this experience of coincidence.

At other times, however, we experience our lives as being unsynchronized with the world around us. On the outside, the world is experiencing a glorious summer while, personally, we are right in the middle of a long winter of "letting-be." Or, the other way around, we are rejoicing in the springtime of "letting-grow" while the trees outside are beginning to lose their leaves.

In a more personal and even more perplexing way, we sometimes find ourselves completely unsynchronized with the people around us. For example, they are enthusiastically celebrating a rite of spring while we are feeling called to "let go" in trust. At times such as these, it is especially difficult to remain faithful to the timing which growing gracefully toward Life requires of us. We are seriously tempted to "join the crowd," regardless of what time it is in our life.

As we learn to remain faithful to our own sense of messianic timing, however, we begin to experience exquisite moments in which the outside timing and the inside timing come together in extremely creative ways. These are moments of special grace and of special full-ness. We know that these moments are not our doing. They are mes-sianic moments in which we experience our lives unfolding in stereophonic time. These are the kind of moment to which the clas-sical tradition refers when it speaks of *kairos:* the "right" or "special" time. They are the kind of moment to which the whole biblical tra-dition refers when it speaks of "the fullness of time." They are the messianic moments in which things start coming together in time.

How much easier growing toward Life would be if we could just buy a clock which tells messianic time! There are no such clocks, however, for messianic time is carried, not by a hair spring, but by a heartbeat. The only way we can learn to tell messianic time is to learn how to listen to the heartbeat of our own life and of all of life. By comparison, learning how to tell solar time is relatively easy. All we have to do is to read the numbers on the clock. Learning how to tell messianic time is a much more difficult, and a much more subtle, task, for it is a matter of learning how to listen to all of life. This is an on-going experiment in which we are engaged for as long as there is time for us in which to grow toward Life by practicing the Art of Pass-ingover.

Passover as a Movable Feast

As our sense of timing begins to change, the meaning of "Pass-over" begins to change for us as well. Before we begin practicing the Art of Passingover, we think of the Passover as a springtime feast in which the Jews celebrate their liberation. We may extend that to the feast of Easter which Christians celebrate at the same time, but that is about as far as it usually goes. As we continue to practice the Art of Passingover, however, we begin to experience the Passover as a movable feast. We realize that it is not limited to any one time or place or type of person. We begin to realize that the Passover is ac-tually being celebrated wherever and whenever anyone is practicing the Art of Passingover by "letting-go" in trust, "letting-be" in hope, and "letting-grow" in love.

For one thing, we begin to experience how the Passover moves through the celebration of the many feasts which mark turning points in growing messianically toward Life. As a Christian, I experience this most powerfully in celebrating the sacraments of our community. When we preach the Word, we are celebrating the Passover, since it is the Passingover of the Messiah which is the kernel of all that we preach. When we celebrate the Eucharist, we are celebrating the Passover, for we are eating and drinking "in memory of him." When we baptize our little children, confirm our young adults, forgive our penitents, marry our lovers, ordain our ministers, anoint our sick and dying, and bury our dead, we are celebrating the Passover; we are marking these messianic moments in our growing toward Life.

As we practice the Art of Passingover, it is astounding how movable a feast the Passover tends to become for us. We begin to see it moving, not only through the major Jewish and Christian feasts, but also through the rituals and feasts of many other peoples, as they, too, mark the moments of their growth toward Life.

Even more marvelously, we begin to notice how the feast of the Passover moves through the lives of individual persons to piece together a messianic community. A father of a family may be "letting-go" in trust, while his wife is "letting-grow" in love, and their adolescent son is "letting-be" in hope. Whether they know it or not, together they are celebrating the Passover, as the whole feast moves not just through their individual lives, but through their life as a community.

This simple example of the Passover moving through a family gives us some idea of how marvelously complex the experience of messianic community actually is. At any given time, the members of a community may be in very different places in their experience of Passingover. It is as they come together to learn how to honor each other's timing and to celebrate their differences that they begin to embody the full mystery of the Passover and become a living celebration of this most movable feast.

In an equally subtle way, we begin to experience how it is that each person can become a living Passover. As we practice the Art of Passingover, we usually experience our lives in terms of one dominant messianic time. We usually experience ourselves as being either in the fall of "letting-go" or the winter of "letting-be" or the spring and summer of "letting-grow."

As we learn to listen more attentively to the many levels of our life, however, we often discover that all the seasons of Passingover are going on in us at the same time. On a physical level, we may be "letting-go"; emotionally, we may be "letting-be"; mentally, we may be "letting-grow." At first, this experience reveals to us how rich, and how subtle, the Art of Passingover actually is. Before long, however, it makes us realize how at any given time each person can be said to personify the whole Passover mystery and to be a movable feast—a person of all seasons.

The Paradox of Happiness

We may begin practicing the Art of Passingover with the expectation that it will just be a matter of time before we are perfectly happy in this world. In fact, our expectation of being perfectly happy is so subtle that it may take us quite a while to realize how all-pervasive it is in our actions. As this dream continues to be postponed, and as our sense of messianic timing becomes more keenly developed, we begin to realize that the perfect happiness which we are seeking is actually beyond time; we carry it in our hearts as a lifelong desire, but it unfolds imperfectly in our lifetime. We find that the happiness we experience in this life always leaves something to be desired; it is always partial and incomplete. It always leaves us with at least one more step to take if we are to continue to grow messianically toward Life. More often than not, that next step hurts.

At first, this experience of unfulfilled hope can be extremely disillusioning. It makes us feel as though we have been duped and made to search for something which cannot be. It makes us want to give up practicing the Art of Passingover altogether. If we stay faithful to the Art of Passingover, however, we begin to realize that our disillusionment is inviting us to recognize what really is, and to embrace a paradox by dedicating our life to pursuing a happiness which can only be imperfectly realized in time. It may seem callous and stupid to say so, but as we grow toward happiness through the Art of

Passingover, we discover that it is a matter of relative indifference whether we are happy or not. What really matters is that, happy or sad, we are growing messianically toward Life. If we are to discover the joy which comes with that, sooner or later we find ourselves "letting-go" of the dream of "perfect happiness here and now" and creatively embracing the paradox of growing toward perfect happiness in less-than-perfect ways. It is in embracing that paradox that we begin to come of age as artists in the Art of Passingover.

In this chapter, we have described the Art of Passingover as an on-going experience of growing messianically toward Life. From this point of view, to practice the Art of Passingover is to live and to let live. We have suggested how our sense of dying, living, timing, Passover and happiness begin to be transformed as we personify the Art of Passingover in this way. Nor is this all that begins to be transformed; the atmosphere in which we live begins to be transformed as well. It starts to become charged with the messianic courage, trust, hope, love and life which it takes to personify the Art of Passingover. These are some of the on-going transformations—the "awesome unfoldings"—which we experience as we continue to "let grow" in love.

From another point of view, we can describe the Art of Passingover as an on-going experience of growing messianically toward Peace. In the next chapter, we turn our attention to this messianic pilgrimage.

Chapter 7

Growing Messianically Toward Peace

Several years ago, I made an extended retreat with a community of hermits who live on a mountain in Big Sur, California. As I spoke with a hermit one day, he told me of three Buddhist monks who had visited the monastery the previous year. They were making a Pilgrimage for Peace from Los Angeles to San Francisco.

"Do you know how Buddhists make a Pilgrimage for Peace?" he asked me.

"No," I replied. "I really don't."

"Well," he said, "the first two monks go on ahead in silence. They take two steps forward. Then they prostrate on the ground. Then they get up, take two more steps forward, and prostrate again. They continue walking in this way for the whole pilgrimage. The third monk walks behind them, ready to explain what the monks are doing, should anyone passing by stop to ask."

The hermit went on to tell me how many of those who passed by had, in fact, shouted obscenities at the monks, thrown garbage at them, and even tried to drive them off the road.

I was appalled and amazed—appalled at the treatment the monks had received, and amazed at the form their pilgrimage had taken. A few days before, I had climbed the road that winds its way up the mountain to the monastery. It had taken me almost an hour. I could not even imagine myself climbing it by taking two steps and then prostrating, much less walking that way from Los Angeles to San Francisco! I found it incredible.

Reactions to the Pilgrimage for Peace

Afterward, I took a long walk on the mountain by myself. The Pilgrimage for Peace would not leave me alone. It kept coming to mind as I walked along.

At first I thought, "How terrible!" I was greatly pained and very angry at those who had abused the monks. It made me wonder whether there was any hope for peace at all among such fast-moving and insensitive people as we Americans sometimes are.

Later I began to think, "How stupid!" Falling down and getting up is no way to make a difference. All it does is give this culture a chance to demonstrate how hopelessly violent it really is.

Much later I began to think, "How extraordinary!" Once again I found myself marveling at the heroic courage, patience, and commitment the monks had shown by continuing on their Pilgrimage for Peace, come what may.

By the time I was returning to the monastery I was thinking, "How extraordinarily ordinary!" I was beginning to realize that what the monks were doing was a symbol of what all of us do when we are committed to moving toward peace in a context of chaos or, for that matter, when we are committed to doing anything of more-than-personal consequence in the world in which we live. We take two steps forward, then fall on our face. Sometimes we fall in anger or despair; sometimes, in failure or exhaustion; sometimes, in prayer and adoration; sometimes, in praise and thanksgiving; but what we do is fall on our face. Then, if we are to keep moving, we get up and take two more steps forward. This seems to be how we make the Pilgrimage for Peace whenever we truly make a Pilgrimage for Peace.

A little later, the Pilgrimage for Peace came to mind again and I found myself remembering the stations of the cross which we used to make as children. Our priest would lead us around the church to twelve sculptures which represented the stepping stones of Jesus' journey to Calvary and, ultimately, to victory. At each of them we would stop and pray a while. I remembered how the three that touched me most as a child were the three which punctuated the whole journey: "Jesus Falls the First Time," "Jesus Falls the Second Time," and "Jesus Falls the Third Time." As we prayed these words we used to kneel down together with our priest. Then, after a moment of silence, we would get up and continue on the way. I did not realize it at the time but, by praying the stations of the cross, we were being taught how to make a Pilgrimage for Peace.

Much later I remembered what I was surprised to have forgotten: a very simple stations of the cross marked the road that made its way up the mountainside to the monastery.

The Art of Passingover as a Pilgrimage for Peace

As we practice the Art of Passingover, we begin to experience our whole lives as a Pilgrimage for Peace. Like the Buddhist monks, we take two steps forward by "letting-grow" in love and doing what has to be done; then we prostrate ourselves by "letting-go" in trust and "letting-be" in hope; then we get up again to "let grow" in love. It is in this seemingly strange way that we begin to discover the pathway that creates peace while we move toward it.

At times along the way, we may well find ourselves saying, "How terrible!" We may be pained and angry to discover how hostile life and others can be as we try to bring peace to a broken world. Without realizing it, we may have been expecting instant results or grateful acceptance; what we experience, instead, is more discord, failure, resentment, and rejection.

We then begin to realize that the Pilgrimage for Peace takes place primarily within our own hearts, and that it must pass through our own human brokenness and vulnerability if it is to find its way toward Peace. We begin to realize that, on the Eighth Day of Creation, the nothingness of human chaos is the ever-present raw material with which we have to work if we are to create a cosmos of peace, and that this nothingness is not merely around us; it is within us. We begin to realize that, as long as we are on Pilgrimage for Peace, both chaos and peace will be our companions.

At times along the way, we may find ourselves saying, "How stupid!" What difference can "letting-go" and "letting-be" possibly make in this hopeless situation? Through half of our lives, we may have become so used to marching straight ahead toward whatever we wanted to accomplish that we may have come to think of that as the only way of getting anywhere. By contrast with that, taking two steps forward and then falling on our face feels stupid; it feels like a good way of getting nowhere, much less to the City of

Peace. Besides, it makes us feel as though we are wounded and limping.

In time we start to suspect that that is how it really is; we *are* wounded and limping. When we begin to admit that we are limping pilgrims, we begin to realize that if Peace is ever to come to this world through us, it will simply have to come from beyond us. We become more sensitive, too, to the escalating cycle of injustice, violence and destruction that the more productive approach of "marching straight ahead" has never failed to create in our lives, and in our world.

As, again and again, we move from thinking that we can never go on, to being given a hidden strength to take still another step toward Peace, we find ourselves saying, "How extraordinary!" Our attention begins to shift from the vision of the City of Peace that we carry in our hearts, to the much more modest task of taking one peaceful step in a chaotic world. It is in this way that both we and the world come to know the way that leads to Peace. As we continue to walk in this way, "How extraordinary!" tends to become our password, for we become more aware than ever of the "awesome unfoldings" which accompany a life dedicated to "letting-go" in trust, "letting-be" in hope, and "letting-grow" in love. These "awesome unfoldings" are like the flowers of peace which spring up along the way of Passingover, even when we ourselves are far from peaceful. Through these wonder-filled experiences, we begin to realize that peace is not the a product of our pilgrimage; it is one of its many by-products. It begins to appear in the most unexpected ways as we continue to dedicate our lives to growing messianically toward Peace by practicing the Art of Passingover.

In time, we begin to personify the Art of Passingover and catch ourselves saying, again and again, "How extraordinarily ordinary." The limping pilgrim's way to Peace becomes natural to us now; we walk it not by making extraordinary gestures, but by doing the ordinary things with extraordinary care. We walk it by carefully taking two steps forward in love, then falling down in trust and hope, then getting up carefully to take two more steps in love again. In this way, step by step, we dedicate our lives to growing messianically toward Peace. "How extraordinarily ordinary!"

The Rhythm of Peacemaking

There is a cadence to this "extraordinarily ordinary" pilgrimage which is very different from that to which an army marches. An army marches to the very purposeful rhythm of, "hut, two, three, four; hut, two three, four." The Pilgrimage for Peace, however, moves to the much less ambitious rhythm of: "one, two, flop; one, two, flop." At first this cadence may strike us as stupid, but as we continue to practice the Art of Passingover, we discover that it is, in fact, a life-giving rhythm which combines loving action with hope-filled repose. Without the hope-filled repose, we forget where we are going and lose touch with the more-than-personal energy and inspiration for getting there. Without the loving action, our heartfelt hopes become wishful thinking which is increasingly unrelated to the realities of our world. It is one thing to be given the vision of the City of Peace in our hearts; it is something else to be given the courage and the energy to walk toward that vision through the chaos of our lives; both are necessary if we are to continue to grow messianically toward Peace. As stupid as it may sound: "one, two, flop; one, two, flop." That is how it goes with pilgrims.

In many monasteries, this inner rhythm for peacemaking is summed up in two Latin words: *Ora* and *Labora,* pray and work. It is this rhythm which establishes the *continuum,* or inner flow, of the monastic way of living in peace. Modern variations on this theme include mottos such as, "Pray and Picket" and "If you desire peace, work for justice." The message, however, remains the same: there is a rhythm in the Pilgrimage for Peace which requires both the repose to receive the gift inwardly, and the work to express it outwardly. While the pacifists for Peace emphasize the importance of the gift, and the activists for Peace emphasize the importance of the work, the rhythm of genuine peacemaking requires them both. The rhythm of peacemaking with integrity is not "flop, flop, flop, flop"; nor is it "one, two, one two"; it is "one, two, flop; one, two, flop." When that rhythm becomes established in our life, it has a way of uniting not only hope-filled repose and loving action, but also the enchantment and the disenchantment which are such an integral part of the Pilgrimage for Peace.

The Enchantment-Disenchantment Cycle

In the eight days following the Easter Vigil, there is a very special kind of teaching which goes on in the daily worship services of the Christian community. This teaching is not intended to prepare the uninitiated for the waters of Baptism; it is intended to prepare the initiated for living the mystery of Passingover. It is a deeply symbolic kind of teaching which sensitizes the more experienced to how the mystery of messianic dying and rising actually unfolds in their own lives. This teaching focuses on the post-resurrection narratives of the Gospel, one of which is the story of the pilgrimage which two disciples make from Jerusalem to Emmaus and back again.

In chapter twenty-four of his Gospel, Luke tells the story of two disenchanted disciples who were walking away from Jerusalem on the Third Day, discussing how their messianic hopes have been crushed by the death of Jesus. In a form which they do not recognize, Jesus joins them. Taking him for a complete stranger, they explain to him how their messianic hopes were crushed by all that had happened during the Passover in Jerusalem.

Undaunted, the stranger chides them for their lack of faith and shows them how clearly the Scriptures attest to the fact that the Messiah will enter into his glory through suffering.

The disciples are deeply moved by the stranger's words and prevail on him to spend the night with them. At supper he takes bread, blesses it, breaks it, and gives it to them. With that they recognize him, and he vanishes from their sight. Elated, they return immediately to Jerusalem. They find the other disciples celebrating the fact that Jesus has been raised from the dead. Then they tell what had happened to them on the road to Emmaus, and how they had recognized him in the breaking of the bread.

At first we might say, "What an extraordinary Pilgrimage for Peace!" Here are two enthusiastic disciples who were thoroughly enchanted with the prospect of the Messianic Peace being fully realized within the "City of Peace." When it does not work out as they had expected, they become thoroughly disenchanted; they turn their backs on Jerusalem and walk away. In this depressed state, they encounter the seemingly ignorant stranger, who not only enlightens them through his words, but also enlivens them through his action.

In a most mysterious way, they are enchanted anew and return again to the "City of Peace" to spread the Good News. In one day's time, they have made an extraordinary Pilgrimage for Peace from Jerusalem to Emmaus and back again.

Since stories have to stop somewhere, this one stops at Jerusalem, the "City of Peace." For most of us, that is fine, since we prefer to think that, after returning to Jerusalem, the disciples lived peacefully ever after. If we think about it a little more, however, we probably know better. It would not be long before disciples like this would be beaten, imprisoned, crucified and thrown to the lions. In all probability, these two enthusiastic disciples still had several equally disenchanting-enchanting round trips to make from Jerusalem and back again before their Pilgrimage for Peace was really over.

As we continue practicing the Art of Passingover, our initial reaction to this story begins to change; we begin to marvel at how "extraordinarily ordinary" this Gospel pilgrimage actually is. We begin to see how clearly it mirrors the on-going cycle of enchantment and disenchantment which is part of any genuine Pilgrimage for Peace. At first we are enchanted by the prospects for achieving Peace in our time, and we get thoroughly engrossed in working for it. Then we get disenchanted by how elusive true Peace is, and how slow it is in coming. This disenchantment is the crucible in which our commitment to Peace is further refined, and in which we are disabused of our personal ambitions and illusions regarding it. In time we become enchanted again as we are energized and missioned from within to take one more step toward Peace. Then something else may happen, and we become disenchanted again . . .

Before long, we begin to realize that the road from Jerusalem to Emmaus is the symbolic pathway to Peace, and that it is designed not for curious tourists, but for dedicated pilgrims. As we make this round trip in our lives again and again, by moving through the cycle of enchantment and disenchantment, we begin to realize that what really matters is not whether we are enchanted or disenchanted, but whether we are growing toward Peace. As others see us continually "letting-go" in trust, "letting-be" in hope, and "letting-grow" in love, they may think that we are losing our mind and moving in circles, but we know that we are moving in cycles of ever-deepening and ever-widening commitment to growing messianically toward Peace.

When we come down to it, that is what the "extraordinarily ordinary" pilgrimage of Passingover is all about.

The Gift of Peace

Ordinarily, when we speak of peace, what we have in mind is the absence of war and hostility. When the biblical tradition speaks of peace, however, it has much more than that in mind. In the Bible, "peace" is a word which symbolizes God's ultimate gift and blessing to his creatures; it is the hallmark of messianic times. From a biblical point of view, to wish others peace is to wish them much more than personal tranquility; it is to wish them perfect well-being. If we were to try to put the full biblical meaning for "peace" into one word, it would sound something like "wholeness-lacking-nothing-life-harmony-family-friends-justice-security-totality-happiness-prosperity-right-doing-Messiah-coming-God-presence-to-one-and-all." Even that mouthful would not express it adequately. However rich they may be, our words and actions can express only a fraction of the richness of *"Shalom."* The reality of *Shalom* is so rich that it takes us a lifetime of dedicated Passingover to get even an intimation of all that it actually means. For as long as we live by Passingover, *Shalom* is the blessing which we carry in our hearts and personify, as best we can, in our lives as we walk with messianic courage through hostile places.

The gift, the work, the courage, and the humility which are at the heart of the Pilgrimage for Peace are reflected in a prayer which sums up the whole dedicated life of Francis of Assisi:

Lord, make me an instrument of Your Peace.
Where there is hatred, let me sow love;
Where there is injury, pardon;
Where there is doubt, faith;
Where there is despair, hope;
Where there is darkness, light;
Where there is sadness, joy.

Divine Master, grant that I may seek
Not so much to be consoled as to console;

Not so much to be understood as to understand;
Not so much to be loved as to love;
For it is in giving that we receive;
It is in pardoning that we are pardoned;
And it is in dying that we are born to Eternal Life.

In the wake of this prayer, we may find ourselves thinking again of the little boy as he approaches his Rabbi.

> "Rabbi," the little boy said, "David tells us in the Psalms that God speaks 'Peace' to his People. Look around, Rabbi, look around. How come God no longer speaks 'Peace' to his People?"
>
> The Rabbi shook his head as though he were in pain. "My son," he replied, "it is not that God no longer speaks 'Peace' to his People. It is that no one these days can stoop down low enough to listen. No one . . . can stoop down low enough . . . to listen."

It is not only in order to listen to such heartfelt murmurings of Peace and to receive such a special blessing, but also to begin to personify and share it, that, in the Art of Passingover, we willingly stoop down very low. We willingly spend a lifetime taking two steps forward, then prostrating, then taking two steps forward again, until we reach the City of Peace.

Since the Pilgrimage for Peace can be a privileged doorway to a messianic experience of Freedom, in the next chapter we will turn our attention to the experience of growing messianically toward Freedom.

Chapter 8

Growing Messianically Toward Freedom

Oh, Freedom. Oh, Freedom.
Oh, Freedom, over me, over me.
And before I'll be a slave,
I'll be buried in my grave,
And go home to my Lord,
And be free.

A Negro Spiritual

Singing of Freedom from Bondage

To sing this haunting refrain is to enter into the soul's deepest yearning for Freedom against the background of human bondage. It is to be invited to become part of a lifelong pilgrimage that leads through bondage to Freedom.

A century ago, the black People of America sang this song with all their heart; to a great degree, they are still singing it today. The black People, however, are by no means the only ones to sing a song like this. In a thousand different tongues, songs of Freedom against the background of human bondage reverberate throughout the course of history. In a thousand different ways, they are songs of Passingover, songs of Exodus. Together, they form the background music—the unending Pilgrim's Chorus—of the human journey. As these songs of Freedom reverberate throughout the whole biblical tradition, throughout all of human history, and within our own personal lives, they tell us that God intends to re-create the world by creating Freedom from bondage through the dedicated lives of courageous persons.

The Journey through Bondage to Freedom

As we sing our own song of Freedom by practicing the Art of Passingover, we begin to realize that Freedom has many faces, each of which is a creative transformation of one of the many faces of human bondage. What is even more, we begin to realize that both the faces of Freedom and those of bondage are different expressions on the face of our own life. This realization may frighten us at first, but that is how it is. In order to recognize what Freedom really looks like, we have to be able to recognize what bondage looks like when we see it written on our own face. As we grow toward bondage, the face of our whole life begins to change; it becomes a face of bondage. As we recoil from that sight and begin to grow toward Freedom, gradually the face of our life begins to change again; it becomes a face of Freedom.

As a man left the President's office one day, Lincoln is reported to have said to the doorman, "I don't like his face."

"Mister President," the doorman objected, "there isn't anything he can do about his face."

"Anyone over forty is responsible for his own face," the President replied.

In this exchange, Lincoln was speaking about much more than the shape of a face. He was speaking about the quality of life that shapes a face; so are we.

1. Growing Toward Bondage

The Art of Passingover is not the only way for us to go about re-creating our world. A much more common way to go about it is to indulge a messiah complex. Rather than stoop low enough to draw on a creative Power greater than our own, we act as though we were God, and make re-creating our world a "do-it-yourself" project that rests solely on our own shoulders. It may take a while for this attitude to establish itself in our lives but, once it does, it begins to enslave us. In very subtle ways, this underlying messianic complex begins to change the face of our life. If we have the courage to continue to look at our face as it changes, we recognize, first of all, that ours is the face of "Something To Prove"; then it is the face of "Something To Hide"; finally it is the face of "Something To Fear." These are the faces of bondage.

The Face of "Something To Prove"

The face of "Something To Prove" is relatively easy to recognize; our jaw is set, our brow is knit, our eyes stare intently ahead, without blinking at all. It is an intense face, a face of great determination, through which we say, "I'll show you"; "I don't need any help"; "Get out of my way."

We get glimpses of this face, from time to time, when we have been hurt, or as we face a special challenge in our lives. Afterward, it tends to go away and our face becomes more relaxed. It is as we respond to hurt and challenge in this way again and again that the face of "Something To Prove" becomes our own. It reflects quite clearly how we look at life, and how life looks to us.

At first, there is something admirable about the face of "Something To Prove." It is a strong face which expresses a growing self-confidence and an emerging sense of our own identity and independence. It is often our face as a young adult, and it is admirable, as far as it goes. The farther the face of "Something To Prove" goes, however, the less admirable, and the more pathetic it becomes. As it ages, the face of "Something To Prove" becomes a face of human bondage.

The Face of "Something To Hide"

The face of "Something To Prove" is a very human face, so it can, and does, change. In fact, as we continue to grow toward bondage, it begins to change dramatically.

We may have done relatively well in emancipating ourselves from our parents and family, in proving our sexual prowess, in putting others in their place, in climbing the corporate ladder, and in establishing ourselves in the world. Then we begin to realize that, in proving ourselves in these ways, we have left a Wasteland rather than a New Creation in our wake.

As we start to note the fall-out and to count the cost of our having something to prove, the face of "Something To Hide" begins to emerge. This is a smiling face which looks quite pleasant at first, but then we realize that there is something inappropriate about our smile. It is a nervous smile. We are forcing it, to cover up what is basically a look of concern and regret. As we look a little closer, we see that this is actually a perplexed, self-conscious face: our brow is furrowed, and our eyes squint, blink, and look nervously away. This is the face of "Something To Hide"; it is a face laced with the fear that others may discover what we have done, whom we have wronged, and what we are hiding. Basically, the face of "Something To Hide" is the face of guilt.

Most of us make a lot of mistakes in the course of growing up, so the face of "Something To Hide" is usually one of our many expressions from childhood on. At first, it, too, tends to come and go. Since it usually takes a lot of living and a lot of "proving it" for us to develop a dominantly guilty face, the face of "Something To Hide" tends to become fully established only in our middle years. By that time, most of us have developed a desperate need for more and more psychic and spiritual closet space in which to hide the less than attractive parts of our lives; this is what the face of "Something To Hide" clearly reflects. It is a face of human bondage.

The Face of "Something To Fear"

The last face to establish itself on the road to human bondage is the face of "Something To Fear." That does not mean that it has not been with us all along; it comes and goes from time to time, whenever we are frightened. It usually takes quite a while, however, for it to become our dominant expression, and a little longer still for us to recognize that "Something To Fear" has become the shape of our own face.

"Something To Fear" is a thoroughly frightened face: our skin is ashen, our mouth hangs open, our eyes stare aimlessly into space, our face becomes a silent scream. As a rule, we can recognize the look of this face from earlier times in our lives, for it is a constant companion of the "do-it-yourself" approach to re-creating the world.

When "Something To Prove" becomes our dominant expression, we live in fear of failure, the competition, or the prospect of our not being as effective as we say we are. When "Something To Hide" becomes our dominant expression, we fear the consequences of what we have done, the reprisal of those whom we have wronged, or the discovery of what we are hiding. It is only as we begin to face the Unknown and the reality of dying that we begin to realize how pervasive fear has been in our lives. It is then that "Something To Fear" becomes our dominant expression; it is the ultimate face of human bondage.

Singing Our Way toward Bondage

Once we have recognized the look of bondage on our own face, it becomes much easier to recognize it on the faces of others.

As we look around in this culture, we find ourselves surrounded by faces of "Something To Prove," "Something To Hide," and "Something To Fear." That should come as no surprise to us since, basically, we are a "do-it-yourself" culture. We idealize the early pioneers and revolutionaries; we admire the self-made woman and the self-made man; we value self-reliance; we advertise and advocate a "do-it-yourself" approach to life. These values build the assumption that, no matter how difficult a task may be, we can do it by ourselves; if it is impossible, it takes us just a trifle longer.

The "do-it-yourself" assumption which is behind much of our action is really put to the test when we are trying not merely to repair an old house or to learn a new skill, but to create a New World of enduring relationships by building an atmosphere of unconditional trust, hope and love in our own lives and in the world around us. Trying to do this really gives us "something to prove." True to form, the more elusive this New World becomes, the longer and harder we tend to work at creating it. In this way, we become latter day Pelagians: workaholics, trying to save ourselves from human bondage and to re-create our world.

As we go about trying to re-create the world on our own and in our own image, we catch ourselves singing the popular song "I Did It My Way." At first we find this to be an enchanting tune. As we sing it over and over again until it becomes the theme song of our life, however, it tends to wear a bit thin. We begin to notice that each time we sing it, we have to sing it a little louder. Before long we are surprised to notice how strident and how grossly overstated our favorite song has become. If we are self-respecting "do-it-yourselfers," this realization not only gives us one more thing to hide, but it also makes us conscious of how many people around us are singing the same tiresome song.

As we get tired of hearing ourself and others singing "I Did It My Way," we may begin wondering to ourself, "Who cares? Am I really making the world any better by doing it my way?" Am I helping the Kingdom come, or transforming the face of the earth and the quality of life by acting in this way? Am I really?" The assumption in our culture is that we are, or we will be very shortly, since we are encouraged to forget that kind of question and just to keep on working and singing, more loudly than ever, "I Did It My Way."

In the long run, "I Did It My Way" is a very different song from "Oh Freedom." It is a freedom song, to be sure, but it is one which, in time, becomes a song of bondage. It is a song which, as we sing it again and again, gradually generates the faces of "Something To Prove," "Something To Hide," and "Something To Fear" in our lives.

2. Growing Toward Freedom

If we finally get tired of singing "I Did It My Way" and start practicing the Art of Passingover, we become familiar with a whole other set of faces. First of all, the face of "Nothing To Prove" emerges, then the face of "Nothing To Hide," and finally the face of "Nothing To Fear." These are the faces which begin to appear as we grow toward Freedom; they are the faces of Freedom.

The Face of "Nothing To Prove"

The first face that emerges, as we practice the Art of Passingover, is the face of "Nothing To Prove." This is the face that comes with "letting-go." As, again and again, we "let go" in trust, the face of our life begins to take on a quality of quiet courage and confidence.

Here and there, there are still clear traces of struggle and pain, but, basically, our face is relaxed and tranquil now; nothing about it is forced, it is soft and receptive. A little smile plays at the corner of our mouth, for we are beginning to be able to laugh at ourselves.

As we begin to practice the Art of Passingover by "letting-go" in trust, the face of "Nothing To Prove" begins to replace the face of "Something To Prove" as our dominant expression. It is the first face of Freedom.

The Face of "Nothing To Hide"

As the face of "Nothing To Prove" gets well established on our journey toward Freedom, another face begins to appear; it is the face of "Nothing To Hide." This face comes from "letting-be" in hope, over and over again, until we are thoroughly at home with the truth of what really is. Our face now becomes one of total attentiveness and expectancy. It carries a curious half-smile. It is a friendly, welcoming, thoroughly open and receptive face. It is a face which quietly waits and wonders about what will come next.

As we practice the Art of Passingover, the face of "Nothing To Hide" gradually begins to replace the face of "Something To Hide" in our life. This transformation happens as we become thoroughly familiar with our own inner hiding places through our experience of "letting-go" and "letting-be." When we described the experience of "letting-be," we spoke of this as a "bombardment from within" through which our dreams, thoughts, and fantasies barrage us with all that is hidden within us. By learning to let that bombardment be, we eventually come to know, better than anyone else in this world, the misgivings, as well as the gifts and mysteries, which lie hidden within us. It is as though we have walked through the closets of our lives a thousand times and have discovered that they are not only hiding places, but also amazing treasure chests. As a result, we no longer hide the facts of our inner lives from ourselves; we are no longer estranged from ourselves and from the Life that moves within us. When we begin to have the experience of "Nothing To Hide" we begin to be liberated in a most radical way; we begin to experience an inalienable Freedom which changes our face from within. We begin singing, and living, a completely new song.

If others look closely, they can recognize the look of "Nothing To Hide" on our face as well. This does not mean that we are given to inappropriate self-disclosure. We know from experience that sort of psycho-spiritual "show and tell" can do tremendous violence to the delicate inner reality of our own lives and the lives of others as well. What the look of "Nothing To Hide" does mean for us is that, in becoming more honest with ourselves, we are capable of being more honest with others; we are capable of sharing with them what we feel, think, regret and treasure, should the integrity of our relationship and growing toward Freedom require it. What is happening to us is that, through the experience of "letting-be," the truth is gradually making us free. It may well be making us miserable first, but it is making us free, nevertheless.

"Nothing To Hide" is a face that becomes ours as we get used to "letting-be" in hope; it is another face of Freedom.

The Face of "Nothing To Fear"

The final face to emerge as we grow toward Freedom through the Art of Passingover is the face of "Nothing To Fear." It, too, is a face that is with us at every phase of Passingover, since every step along the way is an exercise in courage, but it takes a little longer for it to become established as the dominant expression of our life. It is a face that emerges as we go about "letting-grow" in love.

Although it is an older face, the face of "Nothing To Fear" radiates a youthful courage, joy, and vitality. It is a face that knows what it means to live creatively through the experience of dying, again and again. It is a peaceful, benevolent face which carries a quiet smile, even in the most trying situations.

To have the face of "Nothing To Fear" begin to become our own does not mean that we are never afraid again; it means that we have become accustomed to facing our fears, naming them, and being delivered from them, again and again. It means that, as we continue to celebrate the Art of Passingover in our own life, we begin to get the sense that love is continually casting out the fears that hold us in bondage. At first we may not experience this love to be the "perfect love" which Scripture tells us "casts out fear." Later on, however, we may well get the sense that the Love that is working through us and liberating us is, in fact, the perfect Love; it is the Love that is stronger than death. Then we realize that it is no longer our loving, but a bigger-than-personal Loving that is at work in us as we "let grow" in love. At such times we may find ourselves babbling in a Paul-like way, "I love, now, not I, but Love loves in me." Above all, it is the experience of "letting-grow" in such love that transforms the face of our life from "Something To Fear" to "Nothing To Fear." It is hard for a human face to contain a Love such as this, but the face of "Nothing To Fear" does the best it can. It is a face of ultimate Freedom.

Singing Our Way through Bondage toward Freedom

Once we have learned to recognize the expressions of Freedom as they appear on our own face, it becomes relatively easy to recognize them on the faces of others. In fact, it is as we keep remembering the look of Freedom on the faces of others around us that we begin to realize that the faces of "Nothing To Prove," "Nothing To Hide," and "Nothing To Fear" not only reflect Freedom, they create it. By radiating the courage, the hope, and the love which are generated in the Art of Passingover, these faces continually invite us to grow toward Freedom. These are most creative and most supportive faces. They are faces which people and animate our own journey from bondage toward Freedom; they remind us that we do not make this journey alone.

In speaking of the faces of bondage and the faces of Freedom, we have not been speaking primarily of physical faces. We have been speaking of inner faces, of the shape our life begins to take as it faces the task of re-creating the world we live in. It is a good thing to remember that; otherwise we may waste a lot of time looking for some type of "Freedom Cosmetics" with which attractively to make up our face into the face of "Nothing To Prove," "Nothing To Hide" and "Nothing To Fear."

Of course, regardless of how hard we would work at doing that, it would be the faces of bondage that would appear to any discerning

eye, since the faces of Freedom do not come as a cosmetic achievement; they come as gifts which well up naturally from within a life
which is dedicated to the Art of Passingover. While the faces of bondage are generated by a messianic complex, the faces of Freedom are
generated by contact with a messianic Power which is beyond our
own doing. Underneath it all, it is this Power which transforms the
face of "Something To Prove" into the face of "Nothing To Prove" by
en-couraging us in the act of "letting-go"; it transforms the face of
"Something To Hide" into the face of "Nothing To Hide" by filling
us with forgiveness and hope in the act of "letting-be"; and it transforms the face of "Something To Fear" into the face of "Nothing To
Fear" by en-abling us to love through the act of "letting-grow." So,
as we grow toward Freedom, we find that we have nothing to prove,
nothing to hide, and nothing to fear, because we are being en-cour-
aged, for-given, en-trusted, in-spired, en-abled, and en-amored, in
a messianic way, through the Art of Passingover. As we begin to personify the Art of Passingover, more and more "Oh Freedom" becomes our song.

If we think that, eventually, "Oh Freedom" will be the only
song we sing as we grow toward Freedom, and that the faces of Freedom will be our only expressions, we have a bit more Passingover to
do. In the Art of Passingover, Freedom is created from our experiencing the nothingness of our own bondage. As long as we are on the
journey toward Freedom, "Oh Freedom" and "I Did it My Way"
continue to vie for the theme song of our life. As long as we are growing messianically toward Freedom, it is from the look of bondage on
the face of our life that the look of Freedom is created.

This means that, in the Art of Passingover, we have to be forever
attentive to the shape of our face, for it tells us in what direction we
are moving. The faces of "Something To Prove," "Something To
Hide" and "Something To Fear" tell us that we are moving toward
bondage, singing "I Did It My Way" and, perhaps, indulging a messianic complex.

The Faces of Bondage also remind us what time it is in our life.
When we see the look of "Something To Prove" on our face, it tells
us that it is time to "let go" in trust; the look of "Something To Hide"
invites us to "let be" in hope; the look of "Something To Fear" reminds us to "let grow" in love.

When we see the Faces of Freedom beginning to emerge in our life, they tell us that we are growing toward Freedom by embodying the Art of Passingover and that our theme song, once again, is,

> Oh, Freedom. Oh, Freedom.
> Oh, Freedom, over me, over me.
> And before I'll be a slave,
> I'll be buried in my grave,
> And go home to my Lord
> And be Free.

Growing messianically toward Freedom opens us to a very different way of loving, which we will describe in the next chapter.

Chapter 9

Growing Messianically Toward Love

> God is love,
> and whoever lives in love
> lives in union with God
> and God lives in union with him.
> *1 John 4:16*

The Parable of the Prodigal Son

We usually think of the parable of the Prodigal Son as a parable of
forgiveness. It is that, of course, but it is much more than that. It is
a parable of a messianic way of loving. It is a parable of a benevolent
way of loving which is rooted neither in the fulfillment of our personal needs, nor in the real or imagined merits of other persons'
lives, but in the reality of a more-than-personal Goodness. The parable of the Prodigal Son is a lesson in how creative this messianic way
of loving can be. When we listen to the parable in this way, it often
has something very different to say to us:

> There once was a man who had two sons. The
> younger one said to him "Father, give me my share of the
> property now." So the man divided his property between
> his two sons. After a few days the younger son sold
> his part of the property and left home with the money.
> He went to a country far away, where he wasted his
> money in reckless living. He spent everything he had.
> Then a severe famine spread over that country, and he
> was left without a thing. So he went to work for one of
> the citizens of that country, who sent him out to his farm
> to take care of the pigs. He wished he could fill himself
> with the bean pods the pigs ate, but no one gave him any-

thing to eat. At last he came to his senses and said, "All my father's hired workers have more than they can eat, and here I am about to starve! I will get up and go to my father and say, 'Father, I have sinned against God and against you. I am no longer fit to be called your son; treat me as one of your hired workers.' " So he got up and started back to his father.

He was still a long way from home when his father saw him; his heart was filled with pity, and he ran, threw his arms around his son, and kissed him. "Father," the son said, "I have sinned against God and against you. I am no longer fit to be called your son." But the father called to his servants, "Hurry!" he said. "Bring the best robe and put it on him. Put a ring on his finger and shoes on his feet. Then go and get the prize calf and kill it, and let us celebrate with a feast! For this son of mine was dead, but now he is alive; he was lost, but now he has been found." And so the feasting began.

In the meantime the older son was out in the field. On his way back, when he came close to the house, he heard the music and dancing. So he called one of the servants and asked him, "What's going on?" "Your brother has come back home," the servant answered, "and your father has killed the prize calf, because he got him back safe and sound." The older brother was so angry that he would not go into the house; so his father came out and begged him to come in. But he spoke back to his father, "Look, all these years I have worked for you like a slave, and I have never disobeyed your orders. What have you given me? Not even a goat for me to have a feast with my friends! But this son of yours wasted all your property on prostitutes, and when he comes back home, you kill the prize calf for him!" "My son," the father answered, "you are always here with me, and everything I have is yours. But we had to celebrate and be happy, because your brother was dead, but now he is alive; he was lost, but now he has been found."

Luke 15:11–32

The Passingover Experience of the Prodigal Son

There is not just one but there are actually three experiences of Passingover at play in this very moving parable: the Passingover of the younger son, the Passingover of the Father; and the Passingover of the elder son.

The Passingover of the younger son is clearly an experience of repentance on the part of a young man who is bent on growing toward freedom. He does that, at first, by emancipating himself from his father and his father's house, and by going on his own. When it becomes clear that his road to freedom has led him into bondage, he hears his life telling him to "let go" and to return to his father. He obeys and, with his mind filled with a memorized speech and his heart filled with misgivings about what his father's response will be, he walks the awkward way home in hope. Even before he arrives home, the wonder-filled response of his father invites him to let a new relationship, and a completely new life, grow in love. For the younger son, this homecoming celebration marks one full cycle in the Art of Passingover.

The Passingover Experience of the Father

In this cycle of Passingover, the younger son might have learned a lesson in repentance, but that was by no means all that the father was teaching him. The father's own cycle of Passingover is clearly an experience of a most mature kind of loving. Through it, the father is teaching his younger son how to love in a messianic way.

The son's arrogant demand, "Give me the share of the estate that is coming to me," is life's painful invitation to the father to "let go." He no doubt could have thought of some very good reasons for doing otherwise, but he gives the son his share of the property and "lets go" in trust. While the son is making his own way in "a distant land," the father goes through his own agony of "letting-be" in hope. The parable does not tell us this directly, for "the awkward inbetween" of "letting-be" speaks in silence, but we can feel the agony of the father's watchful waiting behind his exuberant experience of "wonder-filled beginning":

> . . . He was still a long way from home when his father saw
> him; his heart was filled with pity, and he ran, threw his
> arms around his son, and kissed him . . .

The father will have none of his son's penitential arrangements; he
does not even let him finish his undoubtedly sincere "servitude
speech." Without looking back at all, he looks toward the next step;
he puts a robe on the young man's back, a ring on his finger, shoes
on his feet, and calls for a celebration. The servants think that the
father is celebrating merely because he has his son back "in good
health," but the father's experience goes much deeper than that. For
him, the journey of his younger son was a Passingover from life to
death and back again. He celebrates because "your brother was
dead, but now he is alive; he was lost, but now he has been found."

The Passingover Experience of the Elder Son

Meanwhile, out in the field, the elder son is not celebrating at
all. He is singing, "I Did It My Way," while envying his brother,
resenting his father, and feeling sorry for himself. Formerly he may
well have loved his younger brother. If he did, it is now clear that
his love was based on how worthy of his love his brother could prove
himself to be. The younger brother failed that test miserably.

Had he heard his brother's "servitude speech," the elder son
probably would have said, "Right on! You *have* sinned against God,
and Dad—and me too! You *don't* deserve to be called Dad's son. You
also don't deserve to be one of his hired hands. And you *certainly*
don't deserve to have a party thrown for you. So get lost, you good-
for-nothing!"

As a middle-aged man, the elder son has a Passingover journey
of his own to make. If he had ears to hear, he would hear an invitation
to "let go" resonating beneath the violence of his emotions. He may
not realize it right away but, by standing in the field all alone, he is
going into exile, just as his younger brother did. In time his life will
start inviting him to "let go" not only of his envy, anger, resentment,
and, perhaps, hatred, but also of his long-standing self-righteous-
ness, so that he may learn to forgive, to understand, and to love in a
completely different way.

The first invitation to Passingover in this way comes when his father goes out into the field to meet him, to assure him that he is loved, and to plead with him to join the party: " . . . we had to celebrate and be happy, because your brother was dead, but now he is alive; he was lost, but now he has been found."

Since the elder son's anger is so fresh, we can well imagine that the father will have to "let go" of him too, and return, heavy-hearted, to the celebration, letting his firstborn be, in hope.

We might imagine as well—as one of my friends once did—that the parable of the Prodigal Son does not stop there:

> Several weeks later one of the villagers stopped the father and asked him what was the reason for the dancing and the music at his house.
>
> "You must join us this evening for the feast!" the father insisted. "We are celebrating, because my son was dead and has come back to life! He was lost and is found!"
>
> "But that was several weeks ago!" the villager objected.
>
> "No," the father replied. "I mean my elder son."

Loving in a Messianic Way

What leads Jesus to tell a parable like this? According to Luke's Gospel, some people could simply not understand what a "Holy Man" like him was doing welcoming sinners and eating with them. Jesus tells the parable of the Prodigal Son in order to help those who are scandalized by what he is doing understand what it means to love in a messianic way. As both the story and the actions of Jesus suggest, this is a way of loving which does not depend on the real or imagined goodness of others; it draws its energy from a much greater Source. It is a benevolent kind of loving, for it sincerely "wishes others well," regardless of how they appear or act. It is a liberating kind of loving, for it does not judge others on the basis of appearances, but enables them to be themselves. It is also a most creative kind of loving, for it transforms apparent evil into transparent goodness, and thereby creates a whole atmosphere in which persons can grow together in

Love. As he packs up and deserts his father, the younger son is not very lovable; as he stands outside in angry judgment, the elder son in not very lovable; yet the father continues to love them both in a messianic way. In the long run, it is this kind of loving that makes all the difference.

The *fruits* of this messianic way of loving are apparent to anyone who has eyes to see and ears to hear: servants dance, neighbors sing, lives are turned around, families are reunited, persons are affirmed, an atmosphere of growth is established, Life is celebrated, and Trust, Hope, Peace, Freedom, Joy, and Love abound. The *roots* of such loving, however, are much less apparent; they reach down past the pain and the power of individual persons and situations into the wellspring of a messianic Love that remains unseen. When the fruits become apparent, we tend to forget about the roots, but that does not mean that they disappear. The roots are always there. It is when the fruits are not yet apparent and when the apparently unlovable are clearly being loved that we begin to wonder how deep the roots of such a love must go. Jesus tells the parable of the Prodigal Son so that those who are scandalized by his way of loving may begin to wonder how deep the roots of messianic loving must go.

When we find ourselves being loved in a messianic way, we too are filled with wonder. We wonder what the other sees in us—whatever it is, we wish that we could see it ourselves! We marvel at how deep such a love can go and at how creative it can be. We begin to suspect that this is a way that surpasses all others, as we experience that,

> Love is patient and kind; it is not jealous or conceited or proud; love is not ill-mannered or selfish or irritable; love does not keep a record of wrongs; love is not happy with evil, but is happy with the truth. Love never gives up; and its faith, hope, and patience never fail.
>
> Love is eternal. . . . Meanwhile these three remain: faith, hope, and love; and the greatest of these is love.
>
> *I Corinthians 13:4–13*

As Paul's experience becomes our own, we begin to experience, not only the story of the Prodigal Son, but also all of Scripture, and all of life, as a parable of messianic loving. We begin to realize that it is in a messianic way that God loves the world.

As we practice the Art of Passingover, we find ourselves, more and more, being loved and loving in a messianic way. We find ourselves being caught up in the way in which the father loves his prodigal son, Jesus loves his followers and detractors, and God loves all of creation. We find ourselves caught up in the way of loving that animates the Eighth Day of Creation by continually "letting-go" in trust, "letting-be" in hope, and "letting grow" in Love.

Loving in a Possessive Way

When we commit ourselves to loving in a messianic way by practicing the Art of Passingover, we are committing ourselves to a way which, in the long run, leads to Freedom. This is by no means the only way of loving, however. There is a possessive way of loving that leads us more and more deeply into bondage. It may be well-intentioned and, at times, very exciting, but, for the most part, it is a passionate kind of loving which has very little in common with the qualities of messianic loving. The hallmarks of its depths are frequently seen to be how impatient, how jealous, how self-seeking, how angry, how indignant, how vengeful, and how fickle it can be. Against a background such as this, the Parable of the Prodigal Son and Paul's ecstatic "Ode in Praise of Love" make no sense at all.

As we indulge ourselves in loving in a possessive way, we usually discover that our love is rooted either in meeting our personal needs or, ultimately, in the illusion that one of us is the Messiah.

When our loving is rooted in the illusion that we ourselves are the Messiah, it frequently takes the form of a not too subtle variation on the theme "I Did it My Way." The variation invariably goes something like, "If You Love Me, Do It My Way." By singing this love song over and over again in a thousand different ways, we learn how to manipulate others and to subjugate them to our own will, by having them continually try to please us and to live up to our expectations. Whether we know it or not, by loving others in this way we continually assume the responsibility for living their lives.

While it clearly enslaves others, this way of loving would seem at least to have the advantage of setting us free. It does not, however. It makes us feel powerful, but it does not make us free. In the long run, it enslaves us by making us increasingly dependent on the dependency of others. In order to indulge the illusion that we are the Messiah, we have to have others who depend on our love.

When our loving is rooted in the illusion that others are the Messiah, we frequently find ourselves loving them by clinging to them. We idealize their goodness to a point beyond belief. We live as though our whole being depends on them. In this way, living and loving comes to mean possessing and pleasing someone else; and so we are led into bondage.

Loving and being loved in a possessive way can feel very stimulating when it is at work at a root level in our lives. As such loving begins to bear its fruit, however, it can be very disillusioning. We begin to realize that these are the fruits of bondage, not of freedom and creativity, and that the roots have been sunk, all along, in personal needs and messianic illusions. As a result, we become greatly disenchanted. It is not uncommon at this time that, in one form or another, we begin to hear the strains of a familiar song:

> Oh, Freedom. Oh, Freedom.
> Oh, Freedom, over me, over me.
> And before I'll be a slave,
> I'll be buried in my grave,
> And go home to my Lord
> And be Free.

If we allow that song of Freedom to start having its way in our lives by practicing the Art of Passingover, we find ourselves getting involved in some of the most trying duets. While others are singing, "If You Love Me, Do It My Way," we begin singing,

> If you love me, let me go;
> If you love me, let me be;
> If you love me, let me grow.

At times, the duet becomes a not-so-harmonious quartet, as others chime in with some variation of "Clinging Is My Way of Loving" and we are called to encourage them to "let go" in trust, to "let be" in hope, to "let grow" in love by doing so ourselves as gracefully as we can.

The Challenge of Loving in a Messianic Way

It is while we are becoming disillusioned with our possessive way of loving that the parable of the Prodigal Son can begin to speak to us again in a stereophonic way. It begins not only to challenge us to love in a different way, but also to show us how to go about it. To accept this challenge is to dedicate ourselves to an on-going lifework, for the journey from loving possessively to loving messianically is not only a long one, it is a recurrent one. It is a journey which we are called to make again and again, as we discover, from time to time, how possessive our loves have become, and how creative they are meant to be. It is a journey which is animated by a trust and a hope which allow the roots of our wayward loving to go so deep that we can begin to love again in a truly messianic, and a most creative way;

> God is love
> and whoever lives in love
> lives in union with God
> and God lives in union with him.
> *1 John 4:16*

In the next chapter we will describe how the experience of growing toward Love opens us to the experience of growing toward God.

Chapter 10

Growing Messianically Toward God

> This is what love is:
> it is not that we have loved God,
> but that he loved us
> and sent his Son to be the means
> by which our sins are forgiven
> *1 John 4:10*

On Being Loved by God

I have always been fascinated by the heliotropism of plants and the theotropism of persons; I have always marveled at how plants unconsciously seek the light and warmth of the sun and how persons unconsciously seek the light and warmth of God's Love. As persons, we do this at the level both of our roots and of our fruits—at a level of both our being and our doing. When we become aware that our roots have been reaching for God all along and that God's Love has been sustaining us throughout, we begin consciously and willingly turning inward toward God in prayer. This moment of prayerful turning marks a major conversion in our life and growth as persons.

It was to mark just such a moment of willingly turning inward toward God that Augustine wrote his *Confessions*. At no place does he better describe what this conversion involves than in the following prayer:

> I have learned to love you late,
> Beauty at once so ancient and so new!
> I have learned to love you late!
>
> You were within me,
> and I was in the world outside myself.

I searched for you outside myself and,
disfigured as I was,
I fell upon the lovely things of your creation.

You were with me,
but I was not with you.
The beautiful things of this world
kept me far from you
and yet, if they had not been in you,
they would have had no being at all.

You called me; you cried aloud to me;
You broke my barrier of deafness.

You shone upon me; your radiance enveloped me;
you put my blindness to flight.

You shed your fragrance about me;
I drew breath
and now I gasp for your sweet odour.

I tasted you,
and now I hunger and thirst for you.

You touched me,
and I am inflamed with love of your peace.

When at last I cling to you with all my being,
for me there will be no more sorrow, no more toil.
Then at last I shall be alive with true life,
for my life will be wholly filled by you.

                    Confessions X, 27–28

Praying as a Way of Loving God

In this passage, Augustine is doing much more than describing
his conversion in a prayerful way. He is groping his way prayerfully

toward God, and revealing how, through his experience of conversion, living and praying have become for him a life-long love affair with the living God.

What a strange affair this is. In being loved by God, Augustine is being loved by Someone whom he cannot see and cannot possess. Yet, in an inward way, Augustine knows that it is God's own Love that is sustaining, calling, enlightening, enamoring, touching, and inflaming him. As a man in his early forties, Augustine realizes, with intense regret, that he has learned to love God late, but he also realizes that it is by no means too late. He now knows how to go about loving an unseen God, by moving prayerfully inward to experience God's Love more intensely, and moving creatively outward to serve God more lovingly.

This recurrent inward-outward movement is the prayer-life cycle which knits together the outside and the inside, the prayer and the work of the mature Augustine. For the rest of his life, he eloquently embodies and advocates this lovingly prayerful, tremendously creative, inward-outward journey for those whom he serves. It is by making this journey over and over again that Augustine celebrates his conversion as a movable feast and becomes a Master in the Art of Passingover.

Praying as an Exercise in the Art of Passingover

I once read a little book which was designed to introduce readers to the art of praying. In it the author described praying as being basically a matter of "going in, staying in, and coming out."

Since then, I have read a lot of books on praying and have done a good deal of praying myself, but everything I have read and experienced has reinforced the simple fact that, as one of the primary ways in which persons grow toward God, praying is basically a matter of "going in, staying in, and coming out"; praying is basically an exercise in the Art of Passingover.

First of all, praying is a matter of "going in"; it is a matter of "letting-go" in trust. "Whenever you pray, go to your room, close your door, and pray to your Father in private. Then your Father, who sees what no man sees, will repay you" (Matthew 6:6). When we pray, we learn to "let go" of whatever is going on around us, so that we may become inwardly attentive to what is going on within us. We may "close our door," or go off by ourselves, or turn off the radio and the television, or close our eyes, or take a walk, or concentrate on our breathing, or focus on an icon, or repeat a special phrase, or work with clay, or sing a chant, or read a favorite text, or listen to music, or find many other ways to begin praying, but what we are doing, basically, is "letting-go" of our everyday activities, concerns and attitudes, so that we may become quiet and inwardly receptive.

After that, praying becomes a matter of "staying in"; it becomes a matter of "letting-be" in hope. More often than not, we no sooner get quiet than a host of things come to mind which seem to be much more important than letting life be in prayer. Praying then becomes a matter of learning to "let go" of these premature invitations to "come out," and of letting the quietness be, in the hope that we too may begin to hear, see, smell, taste, touch, hunger and love in an inward way, and experience the light and warmth of God's Love working at the root level of our lives.

As we begin to experience the reality of being loved by God in an inner way, our great temptation is to "stay in." We begin to feel more and more at home with our inner experiences and less and less inclined to disturb them by returning to the comparatively prosaic, sometimes harsh, realities of our everyday lives. Like Peter on Mount Tabor, we want to pitch our tent at the place of transfiguration. It may seem mean, but praying then becomes a matter of "coming out" so that the energy of God's love which we have experienced in an inner way may find a creative expression in our lives and in our world. In other words, praying then becomes a matter of "letting-grow" in love. The water in the wellspring of praying is meant for the flowers.

This "going in, staying in, coming out" approach to the experience of praying seems to apply to communal prayer as well as it does to personal prayer. Whether it be by welcoming, washing, singing, repenting, or just becoming quiet, any form of communal praying that I know begins with a "going in" rite of some sort or other. Then there is a communal way of "staying in," whether it be by sharing silence, or chanting, or dancing, or reflecting on the Word, or celebrating a sacred ritual of some sort. Finally, there is usually some communal way of "coming out," or missioning, in the hope that the fruits of the common prayer may be shared with others.

Not one but two conversions are involved in this experience of prayerful Passingover. There is a conversion of our flow of energy from the outside to the inside of our lives through "letting go," and a subsequent conversion of our flow of energy from the inside to the outside in "letting grow." This double conversion of Passingover carries the basic movement of the cycle of praying. If we keep this cycle going for any length of time, it becomes an undeniable fact of our experience that there are two sides—an inside and an outside—to the story of both our personal and our communal lives, and that the story is basically incomplete unless we are in touch with both sides of it.

The Creative Rhythm of Praying

As we practice the Art of Passingover by praying, we become more accustomed to the recurrent inward-outward movement of praying and a basic rhythm begins to establish itself in our prayer. It is a rhythm which moves from being active, to being passive, to being active again.

As we "go in," we are actively involved in "letting-go" of what keeps us closer to the surface of our lives and in doing the things which help us move inward. When we learn to "stay in" by letting our inner experiences be, our praying gradually becomes increasingly passive and receptive. At length, it is as though we are no longer praying; we *are* the prayer. We are no longer "doing"; we are simply "being." We are no longer loving God; God is loving us. As we begin to "come out" by "letting-grow" in love, our praying becomes more active again.

Both in our personal and in our communal experience of praying, this delicate interplay between being active and being passive marks the essential rhythm of the praying cycle and the basic dynamic through which it moves us gradually and lovingly forward toward God.

Experiencing the Mystery of Benevolent Loving

In moving prayerfully toward the experience of God's Loving, we are moving into the experience which animates our life at its tap-root level; we are moving into the Mystery which grounds our being. Regardless of how deep our prayer may go, God's Loving remains a mystery to us, not because we cannot experience it, but because, having experienced it, we can neither comprehend it fully, nor express it adequately. All we know is that it is happening. In fact, it is such a subtle experience of loving that, at times, we do not even know that. At its deepest level, the experience of God's Loving is, and remains, ineffable; it takes place in the silent, "letting-be" depths of our lives where God lets us be simply by loving us. To experience God's Loving at this level is to experience the Life beneath all life, the Gift beneath all gifts, the Good beneath all goodness, the Beauty beneath all beauty, the Truth beneath all truth, the Energy beneath all energy, and the Love beneath all loving. This is such a unique experience of being loved unconditionally that it strikes us as unlike anything else in the world.

As the experience of being loved in this way becomes an undeniable part of our experience of Passingover in prayer, we begin to develop a certain sense of kinship with those who refuse to speak directly of the experience of the Mystery. We begin to understand the disciple when he answers his Zen Master's question "And what do you hear now?" with a bow and a smile. We begin to understand what Lao Tse means when he says, "Those who know do not speak; those who speak do not know." We begin to understand what the medieval monk means when he says that a little cloud of unknowing is always between God and us in prayer. We begin to understand why some pious Jews refuse to pronounce the Holy Name and spell it only partially. We begin to understand why Buddhists speak of the experience of Enlightenment only with the greatest reluctance and in the most paradoxical ways. We begin to understand why the prophetic tradition looks with such suspicion on images or observances which may create the illusion that the Mystery of God's Loving can be comprehended, possessed, controlled or manipulated by us. We begin to understand the "learned ignorance" of the sages of the desert when they say, "Seek God, not where he lives." We begin to understand why a genius like Thomas Aquinas would consider all his learned writings to be straw after a personal experience of the Mystery. We begin to understand why the Christian tradition has always celebrated the Mystery of Life and its unfoldment with symbolic words and symbolic actions. It is as though we become part of an invisible communion of those who are aware that their lives are animated by the Ineffable.

In addition, we begin to see how the rest of our experience of praying is either a prelude or a postlude to the ineffable experience of being loved by God. We start to appreciate how all of our praying either leads to this experience or leads from it. As we look back, we can see how our whole experience of "going in" serves to wean us away gradually from equating God and God's Loving with any thing, or place, or thought, or concept, or image, or feeling, either outside or inside of us. We now understand why the experience of "going in" strikes us as so negative at first. We see that as it gradually invites us to "let go" on progressively deeper levels of our lives, the experience of "going in" becomes a constant recognition of "not here," "not there," "not this," "not that"; for the God whose love we experience in "letting-be" is literally "No-thing," "No-one," "No-where." We also begin to see how our whole experience of "coming out" is an attempt to find some creative, symbolic, albeit token expression for what happened to us in the awesome "in-between" of "letting-be." This prayerful experience of being loved by God gives us the vantage point of the Eighth Day of Creation; it allows us to look at all of creation and to affirm both that it is good, and that the Goodness of God transcends it to an Infinite degree.

As we experience praying as an exercise in the Art of Passingover, it becomes much more for us than "saying our prayers." It becomes an on-going experience of "letting-go" of our misconceptions of God and of God's Loving, of letting the experience of God's Loving be within us, and of letting the reality of God's Loving grow through us. In light of this experience we find ourselves beginning to understand, not only what Augustine is saying, but also what he is experiencing as he describes the wonder-filled unfoldment of his own growth toward God:

But what do I love when I love my God?

Not material beauty or beauty of a temporal order;
not the brilliance of earthly light, so welcome to our eyes;
not the sweet melody of harmony and song;
not the fragrance of flowers, perfumes, and spices;
not manna or honey;
not limbs such as the body delights to embrace.
It is not these that I love when I love my God.

And yet, when I love him,
it is true that I love a light of a certain kind,
a voice, a perfume, a food, an embrace;
but they are the kind that I love in my inner self,
when my soul is bathed in light that is not bound by space;
when it listens to sound that never dies away;
when it breathes fragrance that is not borne away on the wind;
when it tastes food that is never consumed by eating;
when it clings to an embrace from which it is not severed
by fulfillment of desire.
This is what I love when I love my God.

But what is my God?
I put my question to the earth.
It answered "I am not God,"
and all things on the earth declared the same. . . .
Clear and loud they answered, "God is he who made us."
I asked these questions simply by gazing at these things,
and their beauty was all the answer they gave.

Then I turned to myself and asked, "Who are you?"
"A man," I replied. . . .
And I know that my soul is the better part of me,
because it animates the whole of my body.
It gives it life,
and this is something no body can do for another body.

But God is even more.
He is the Life of the life of my soul.

Confessions, X, 6.

On the one hand, negation: "not this, not this, not this." On the other hand, transcendent affirmation: "like this, like this, like this—to a more-than-personal, messianic degree." And inbetween, an ineffable experience of loving and being loved by God.

The Prayer-Life Cycle

When we first start praying, we may think of praying merely as a matter of "saying our prayers." In that case, we usually think of praying as being one thing, and of living as being something else. When we begin to realize that praying is actually a mini-experience of the Art of Passingover, however, the dichotomy between praying and living begins to break down. We begin to experience praying and living as mirror images of one another. Our praying becomes a micro-experience of living and our living becomes a macro-experience of praying. We find that living and praying become two sides of our story moving us back and forth from one to the other; living leads us to praying more deeply and praying leads us to living more creatively. We also find that praying and living both move in the same way; both are reflections of the messianic life cycle of Passingover. Both move and grow by our "letting-go" in trust, "letting-be" in hope, and "letting-grow" in love. With that, we begin to experience praying and living as so interrelated that at times it is hard for us to distinguish them. In fact, we may find ourselves wondering why we were so concerned about trying to distinguish them in the first place.

The Stages of the Prayer-Life

The last temptation of the Buddha was not to try to share his ineffable experience of enlightenment for fear that no one would understand. The last temptation of those who experience God's transcendent Loving in this life is to think that they have attained the goal of growing toward God, and that the Art of Passingover is finally over. Furthermore, a casual acquaintance with the classical descriptions of how the life of prayer, and the prayerfully animated life as a whole, unfold serves to reinforce this temptation.

Classically, the life of prayer is said to move from *lectio* to *meditatio* to *contemplatio:* it is said to move from reading God's Word in a stereophonic way, to being infused with an understanding of the mysteries underlying it, to being completely enraptured with God.

The prayerfully animated life is seen to unfold in a similar way, as it moves from a *purgative,* through an *illuminative,* to a *unitive* stage. In the purgative phase, we are purged of our penchant for wrong-doing and of our inordinate attachment to things and persons, and are given a sense of the pathway inward. In the illuminative phase, we are purged of our attachment to our personal ways of knowing and judging and are given an intuitive sense of God's way of seeing things. In the unitive phase, we become so enamored and transformed by God that it is almost as though we ourselves are completely phased out. At the root level of our lives, we are purged of all that is purely personal and gifted with a more-than-personal experience of God Loving.

Thumb-nail descriptions such as these may lead us to believe that, after we have experienced contemplation in praying and the transforming union in our growing toward God, there is no further step for us to take. Of course, neither a more nuanced understanding of these classical descriptions of spiritual growth, nor the lives of those from whom they are derived, will validate this misconception. To experience God Loving is to experience a Power which not only transforms us, but which also energizes us to assist in creatively transforming the world in which we live. To experience contemplation or transpersonal union is to experience a gift which wants to become an artwork and a lifework. As we begin to realize that, the Art of Passingover continues to go on.

This little Zen story speaks clearly to the importance of taking the "coming out" step on the other side of deeply contemplative and transforming spiritual experiences:

A disciple once came to his Master and said, "Master, I am enlightened! What do I do now?"

The Master replied, "Fetch water and chop wood."

We can imagine how perplexed the disciple is by this reply. He has reached enlightenment! He seems to think that that is what the discipline of Zen is all about. He may also think that fetching water and chopping wood is now beneath his dignity. With the goal of the whole discipline achieved, he is wondering whether he has been phased out of a job!

At first the Master's reply strikes us as enigmatic. Later on, however, we begin to realize that the Master is actually saying, "Do the next ordinary thing which Life requires, my son, for Zen is not merely about being enlightened; it is about doing ordinary things with an extraordinarily creative mindfulness." In other words, as the Buddha's own life attests, Zen is not only a matter of "going in" meditatively; it is also a matter of "coming out" creatively.

The same becomes true for us, as we continue to grow messianically toward God:

We love
because God first loved us.
If someone says he loves God,
but hates his brother,
he is a liar.
For he cannot love God, whom he has not seen,
if he does not love his brother, whom he has seen.
1 John 4:19–20

As our practice of the Art of Passingover leads us from growing inwardly toward God in prayer to living creatively in this world, it brings us back to the invitation with which we originally began these reflections. So we will devote our final chapter to describing the experience of growing messianically toward a New Creation.

Chapter 11

Growing Messianically
Toward a New Creation

I consider that what we suffer at this present time cannot
be compared at all with the glory that is going to be re-
vealed to us. All of creation waits with eager longing for
God to reveal his sons. For creation was condemned to lose
its purpose, not of its own will, but because God willed it
to be so. Yet there was the hope that creation itself would
one day be set free from its slavery to decay and would
share the glorious freedom of the children of God. For we
know that up to the present time all of creation groans with
pain, like the pain of childbirth. But it is not just creation
alone which groans; we who have the Spirit as the first of
God's gifts also groan within ourselves as we wait for God
to make us his sons and set our whole being free.

Romans 8:18–23

An Invitation to the Eighth Day of Creation

What a difference between the biblical description of how the first
days of creation unfold, and this most vivid picture of how the Eighth
Day of Creation unfolds. Through Paul's eyes, we can see the New
Creation coming into being through our own labor pains. We can see
it coming into being, as we groan together with all of creation in one
great act of giving birth to a completely glorious embodiment of
God's creative intention. Nor are we the only ones whom Paul hears
groaning in this most creative act; he also hears God's creative Spirit
groaning within us: "The Spirit too helps us in our weakness, for we
do not know how to pray as we ought; but the Spirit himself makes
intercession for us with groanings that cannot be expressed in
speech" (Romans 8:26).

In these passages, Paul is not speculating about the world's and his own radical brokenness and incompleteness; he is experiencing it intensely. He is experiencing the world, as he knows it, coming to an end. That is not all that he is experiencing, however; he is also experiencing a messianic hope that a completely New Creation will come out of these ruins and a messianic conviction that it will come by our growing through chaos.

In sharing this vision of the Eighth Day with us, Paul is inviting us to join him in growing messianically toward a New Creation. He is inviting us to grow toward an integrity which is beyond our own doing by entering willingly into the labor pains of our own lives with more-than-personal courage and vision.

The Cycle of Messianic Creativity

Paul does much more than invite us to live creatively, however; he personifies how we can go about it. The above text shows that his response to the chaos he experiences in himself and in the world around him is in fact a stereo response of compassion, contemplation, communion, and creative commitment which corresponds directly to the word which ushers in creation's Eighth Day: "Let go; Let be; Let grow." Paul's fourfold response patterns for us the whole cycle of messianic creativity through which we grow toward a New Creation.

First of all, Paul's response to his experience of the chaos of creation is one of *compassion:* he "suffers-with" the world. At one and the same time, he celebrates its beauty and laments its corruption. Moved by such compassion, Paul begins to "let go" of all that characterizes his old self and this broken world.

Paul's second response to creation is one of *contemplation:* he "takes it to heart" in all of its beauty and brokenness, until the messianic vision of a New Creation begins to emerge from its nothingness. He "lets it be" in hope.

Paul's third response to creation is one of heartfelt *communion:* in an inward way, he is at-one in the Spirit with all of creation and with all who join it in giving birth to its next phase.

Paul's fourth response to creation is one of *creative commitment:*

he dedicates his life to letting the messianic vision of a New Creation grow in love, until he and the world are spiritually transformed.

In this fourfold response to creation, Paul personifies the integrating cycle of messianic creativity as it moves from compassion to contemplative vision, to spiritual communion, to creative activity. He also personifies the messianic courage it takes to remain faithful to every phase of this creative cycle.

Breaking the Cycle of Messianic Creativity

Of course, remaining faithful to every phase of the cycle of messianic creativity is not our only option. We can break the cycle of creativity at any point along the way.

For one thing, we can respond to the chaos which we experience in ourselves and in the world around us in other than a compassionate way. We can deny it and hope that it will go away. We can pretend, in an increasingly nervous way, that everything is "Fine, fine, just fine." We can let it overwhelm us. We can let it frustrate us. We can begin to blame others for it, and start cursing everyone and everything, including God. We can substitute an endless cycle of cursing for the messianic cycle of creativity and wind up, not only cursing ourselves, but also personifying the disintegration of creation.

Furthermore, we can always respond to our own and the world's radical brokenness in other than a contemplative way. We can panic. Rather than "taking it to heart," we can "fight it." We can rush around, without a vision, "working at it," "fixing it," until we fall over in exhaustion and realize that what we have created is only more personal and cosmic debris—in our own broken image and likeness.

Finally, we can always respond to the contemplative vision of a New Creation and the experience of inner communion in a way other than that of creative commitment. We can let the stark contrast between the heartfelt vision of a New Creation and the heart-rending brokenness in which it actually unfolds infatuate us with the reality of the vision and make us oblivious of the reality of the brokenness. Paul knew this temptation only too well. In a letter to his friends at Corinth, he alludes to the messianic vision which changed his whole life, and adds:

But to keep me from being puffed up with pride because of the many wonderful things I saw, I was given a painful physical ailment, which acts as Satan's messenger to beat me and keep me from being proud. Three times I prayed to the Lord about this and asked him to take it away. But his answer was: "My grace is all you need, for my power is strongest when you are weak." I am most happy, then, to be proud of my weaknesses, in order to feel the protection of Christ's power over me. I am content with weaknesses, insults, hardships, persecutions, and difficulties for Christ's sake. For when I am weak, then I am strong.

2 Corinthians 12:7–10

This experience taught Paul that he was not to romanticize the messianic vision of a New Creation; he was to embrace the paradox of its being realized through human weakness. In responding as he did, he is personifying for us how we can do the same. As we have seen, however, there are many ways in which we can disregard this invitation and break the cycle of messianic creativity; there are many ways in which we can become less and less creatively involved with the chaos that envelops us.

Passingover as a Creative Art

We may not think of ourselves as creative persons but, as we practice the Art of Passingover, we are often surprised to find ourselves at home in the company not only of Paul, but also of many other extremely creative persons. This does not happen through our using their words or imitating their lives. It happens through our making the same moves in our own lives as they did in theirs; it happens as we live our lives as fully as we can, by "letting-go" in trust, "letting-be" in hope, and "letting-grow" in love. As we do this, we find our circle of creative friends becoming broader and broader. It is as though we become part of an anonymous guild—or, better yet, communion—of artists in Passingover which stretches back through all time. As time goes on, this sense of shared creativity becomes an increasingly important part of the Art of Passingover. It becomes part of its "awesome unfolding" and assures us once again that, in Passingover, we are never truly alone.

As we live through the cycle of Passingover again and again, our own response to life, and to the world in which we live, becomes increasingly one of *compassion, contemplation, communion,* and *creative commitment;* we learn to "suffer with" our experience; to "take it to heart" until we are given a vision of what it truly wants to become; to be at-one with its inner possibilities; and to commit ourselves to expressing that inner vision and those inner possibilities in the world as best we can. In this way, we begin to personify the messianic cycle of creativity.

It is easy for us to underestimate, at first, the real importance of this recurrent cycle of creative experience. By comparison with the great achievements of our more celebrated artist friends, that is, with the *things* they did, living through this apparently modest messianic cycle of creativity again and again can seem quite pedestrian. In fact, we may be so accustomed to equate art with artifacts that we may not even recognize that the *process* of Passingover is a work of art in itself. We may be so accustomed to equate art with *things* that we may not even notice what is beginning to happen to our *person* and to the *atmosphere* in which we live as we go about practicing the Art of Passingover.

Whether we notice it or not, however, as we practice the Art of Passingover, the atmosphere of our own lives and of our immediate environment begins to become charged with messianic creativity. It begins to be transformed from whatever it was before into an atmosphere of compassion, contemplation, communion, and creative commitment; it begins to be transformed into an atmosphere of more-than-personal courage, trust, hope and love in which persons can live truly creative lives. These qualitative changes in the personal atmosphere of the world are among the classic signs of messianic times. No matter how modestly, or unconsciously, we may be involved in helping to generate them, in doing so we are involved in the messianic task of bringing a New Self and a New Creation to birth.

We may well count Jeremiah, Beethoven, Michelangelo, Dorothy Day, Hammarskjöld, Mother Teresa and Gandhi among our most creative friends. We may also admire *what* these persons were able to accomplish in their lives more than we admire anything we ourselves have ever been able to do. It is by comparing ourselves with others in this way that the best becomes the enemy of the good.

When we meet the Messiah, he does not ask us whether we are becoming Jeremiah, Beethoven, Michelangelo, Dorothy Day, Hammarskjöld, Mother Teresa, or Gandhi. He asks us whether we are becoming our true self, for that is our most creative task, and the most radical way in which we can make a creative difference in the world. More often than not, becoming their true self is what our most creative friends are about in the first place.

In time, we begin to realize a truth that is at the heart of Passingover all along: the art of living is the most creative art of all. Once we have realized that, we begin to understand how our circle of friends comes to include such celebrated artists. By "letting-go" of what was in their art, by envisioning what could be and what no one had envisioned before, and by dedicating their lives to expressing that vision as faithfully and as skillfully as they could, they model for us, in a very dramatic way, what it means, and what it takes, to live creatively.

As we begin to realize to what degree the Art of Passingover is involved in any truly creative activity, we find that the categories by which we customarily distinguish art from the rest of life begin to break down. We begin to see that any work in which we are dedicated to giving outward expression to a heartfelt vision is, in fact, an artwork in progress, and a piece of the master artwork of living creatively.

As we go about the ordinary tasks of living in the frame of mind that any of them can become an integral part of the messianic artwork of our lives, we find not only the quality of these tasks beginning to improve, but also some very creative things beginning to happen on the side. For the most part, we do not plan them; they just happen through us. More often than not, they come to us as a surprise. They come as unanticipated by-products of our dedication to the artwork of living our lives with integrity; they come to us as we practice the Art of Passingover. They are part of our experience of "awesome unfoldment" as we go about "letting-grow" in love.

From Misery to Ministry

As with any form of art, it is easy to idealize the Art of Passing-over—especially when we are not practicing it ourselves. It is easy to become rhapsodic when we see someone else's dedication beginning to bear fruit.

When we are practicing the Art of Passingover ourselves, however, the fruits of our labors find their proper place in an on-going cycle of enchantment and disenchantment, and in a creative process that is continually working with human chaos, nothingness, and brokenness. It is easy for the casual observer to forget, but what we are invited to work with creatively, in the Art of Passingover, is the chaos of our own and the world's disintegration, alienation, indifference, fear, bondage, mindlessness, suspicion, arrogance, despair, hatred and death. We are invited to work creatively with the cosmic fall-out of our own and the world's disintegration; this is the raw material from which the New Creation comes. When we find compassion, mindfulness, communion, respect, commitment, courage, pardon, trust, integration, freedom, hope, love and new life being generated from within such an environment, we know that something truly creative—and genuinely messianic—is going on.

In the work that I do, I have a lot of contact with persons who are creatively involved in helping others. Whenever I have the opportunity, I like to ask them how they came to be doing the work to which they are so clearly dedicated:

"How did you ever get involved in marriage counseling?" I ask.

"Our marriage was falling apart," they answer. . . .

"What drew you to working with abused children?" I ask.

"I was an abused child," she answers. . . .

"What led you into teaching macrobiotic dieting?" I ask.

"I was dying of cancer, and it saved me," he answers. . . .

"How did you become involved with drug and alcohol rehabilitation work?" I ask.

"I am a recovering alcoholic," she answers. . . .

"It is awfully kind of you to visit prisoners like that," I say.

"I was a prisoner once, myself, you know," he answers. . . .

Of course, there are many who are led to a creative work

through the more conventional channels of being missioned by a church or synagogue, or by marveling at someone who did the work with special dedication, but I am struck by the number of persons who are led to undertake a most creative work through their experience of their own and the world's deep misery. I am also struck to find how spontaneously their life leads them to move from the initial experience of misery to some form or other of soul-searching or meditation, and through that to an experience of mystery, or the more-than-personal depths of their lives, before they are led from there to the work which they feel called to do. Even though they may not use the words, in moving from *misery*, to *meditation*, to *mystery*, to *ministry*, these persons are, in fact, moving from compassion, to contemplation, to communion, to creative commitment.

Afterward, they have no trouble telling me how they came to do what they are presently doing; as they are moving through *misery to meditation*, however, they usually have no idea of what is happening to them, or of where their life is leading them. They are hurting and scared to death. As the cycle completes itself by moving from *mystery to ministry*, however, it is as though their pain reveals its purpose. All along, it meant to teach them how to be true to themselves, how deep their spiritual resources go, how to be true to a Power beyond themselves, and how to serve others creatively with compassion. What went down in pain, then, comes up in praise; what went inward in suffering comes outward in service. *What* these persons wind up doing is usually very obvious and very creative, especially to the persons whom they serve. *How* they originally moved from misery to meditation, to mystery, to ministry, and how they continue to do so, however, is much less obvious, but even more creative. This is the artwork beneath all of their creative work; it is the way in which they practice the Art of Passingover.

Anonymous Ministers

Unless we are formally trained, ordained, and missioned by a specific religious community to serve its people, many of us do not think of ourselves as being called to ministry.

There is another sense, however, in which each of us is called to ministry. If our life is going to go on in any meaningfully human way, each of us is called to care for ourselves, for others, and for the world in which we live. To be called to ministry, in this sense, is to be called to find our métier; it is to be called to find a heart-felt work through which our lives can be connected to a more-than-personal Power and can be of some service to others and the world. It is to be called to find the work through which we can live creatively care-filled lives. Apart from such a work, we experience our lives as meaningless and our actions as making no difference. Before long, we start living and acting in that way, and our lives and the world around us begin falling apart. When this starts happening to us, we may begin to suspect that being engaged in a meaning-filled lifework is a ministry to which each of us is called.

The curriculum which most of us follow in trying to find our métier is not one which a seminary provides for us; it is one which Life itself gives us. It is a curriculum through which Life teaches us the Art of Passingover by leading us to move, again and again, from misery, to meditation, to mystery, to ministry in our own lives.

The integrity of this curriculum of Passingover is reflected in the word "métier" itself. "Métier" is a word rooted in two ancient Latin words: "*misterium*" meaning mystery, and "*ministerium*" meaning activity, or work. To find our métier, then, is to discover a work that has deep, life-giving meaning for us and the world. It is to experience a mystery that wants to become a ministry through which we can grow toward a New Creation.

This Life-given, rather than school-given, curriculum applies for most ordained ministers, as well. It is true that the seminary is the "seedbed," or nursery, in which their first call to ministry is carefully nurtured; but it is often not until much later that they find the form that their métier—their lifework—is meant to take. It is frequently then that their lives and their ministry become most creative. Inbetween, Life usually goes about trying to teach them how to move gracefully from misery, to meditation, to mystery, to ministry, by "Letting-go" in trust, "Letting-be" in hope, and "Letting-grow" in love.

As we begin to appreciate this universal call to ministry, we begin to realize that the Art of Passingover is, in fact, a messianic rite of ordination and missioning. Through it we are missioned, or sent, inward from "letting-go" in trust to "letting-be" in hope, and then missioned outward from "letting-be" in hope to "letting-grow" in love. Through it we are missioned inward from compassion to contemplation, and missioned outward from communion to creative commitment. Through it we are missioned inward from misery to meditation, and missioned outward from mystery to ministry. As we practice the Art of Passingover we find that, at the deepest level of our lives, this inward-outward missioning is the two-fold conversion which becomes our own *curriculum vitae;* it becomes the way in which we are personally ordained and missioned to grow messianically toward a New Creation.

At first, we may ask ourself, "What good is it to be an anonymous minister? What good is it to be a minister if no one else knows that I am one?"

Later on, we begin to realize that others do not have to know about it; if we and Life know about it, that is more than enough. We begin to realize that it is by living it out in an anonymous way that the messianic secret, mystery, and power of our ministry is best preserved. In the end, it is the revelation of this mystery that Paul sees all the world to be waiting for. In the meantime, as we go about living more and more from our experience of the mystery, others may think that we are "just" raising a family, or "just" running a business, or "just" making music, or "just" cooking meals, or "just" building houses, or "just" teaching literature, or "just" farming, or "just" doing any of the many things that we are doing with inner dedication. So be it. We know better. We know that we are Passingover from death to life. In the long run, that is what really counts.

Work in Search of a Soul

The great temptation in our extraverted culture is to overlook the inward move to meditation and mystery, and to equate our métier, or lifework, simply with what we do or produce. When we succumb to this temptation, our work begins to lose its meaning, and we begin to lose heart. Since we are an industrious people, we Americans may respond to that by working harder and harder, but the harder we work, the more meaningless our work tends to become.

In time our work no longer energizes us; it exhausts us. We bring little or no vision and creativity to it. Although we may not be willing to admit it, our work has become a "job" in which we have lost interest. Our primary interest now is not in doing our work with integrity, but in the extrinsic compensations, benefits and rewards we receive for putting up with it. Before long we are either making all kinds of excuses for working poorly or not at all, or we are working so compulsively that we are on the road to burnout.

The American business community is finding the above scenario all too common these days. It is currently facing a crisis of meaning, vision, and creativity in the workplace. Drawing on the Japanese approach to work, some American experts in organizational development are even going so far as to advocate a "spirituality of the workplace" so that the world of work may be fully humanized, and persons may be energized, rather than depleted, by the work they do. It is not surprising to find these experts recommending that time for personal relaxation, meditation, and reflection be included in the ordinary rhythm of the workday as basic ways in which work can be humanized, take on an inner meaning, and once again, become creative. In other words, these are basic ways in which our work can, once again, find its soul.

Ministry in Search of a Soul

As strange as it may seem, many American religious communities are facing the exact same dilemma in ministry these days as the American business community is facing in work. Our culture's excessively extraverted and self-confident approach to work is particularly devastating as it applies to ministry. It leads us to equate ministry with the part of the work that is outside of us, and to forget about the part that is within us. It also leads us to equate ministry with service to others, and to overlook its vital roots in the lives of individual persons. In effect, our exclusively extraverted approach to ministry invites us to by-pass the messianic cycle and rhythm of creativity.

Our cultural bias toward extraversion is only intensified by the crisis in ministry which many religious communities are currently experiencing. In many religious communities these days, there is more and more work to be done, and fewer and fewer ministers to do it. This situation puts tremendous pressure on the ministers who are still active. The demands on their time and energy are so great and so constant that these ministers take less and less time to pray and to care for themselves. The Sabbath, and every other day, becomes an endless workday for them. In an effort to respond to the growing needs, they move directly from misery to ministry, with little or no time for anything inbetween. In this way, they short-circuit the messianic cycle of creativity. Their work and their lives become increasingly frantic. They bring less and less energy, vision, creativity, and compassion to their ministry.

Ironically, as it begins in this way to lose its soul, their ministry itself starts to become their misery. It is not long before they find that what was once a work of dedication is now a "drag"; what once lent a more-than-personal meaning to their own and others' lives is now an impossible "job." They then start either looking elsewhere to compensate for the meaninglessness of their ministry, or working harder and harder with less and less inspiration and vision, until they burn themselves out.

The experience of burnout is especially painful for ministers. They are often expected not only to "have it all together" but also to be superhuman. After a while, some ministers even begin to expect this of themselves. At any rate, they are persons who have committed themselves, in a public and highly visible way, to helping others, and now it is clear that they are hurting, broken, and badly in need of help themselves. Even if no one says it, ministers in this position begin to hear, "Doctor, cure yourself."

The experience of their own brokenness and of their inability to cure themselves can be the end of the road for once effective ministers, or it can be the beginning for them of a qualitatively new experience of religious life and ministry. It is at this breaking point of personal and spiritual burnout that Life begins to reveal its own curriculum, by inviting them to "let go" in trust, and by missioning them inward to learn, once again, to take their lives and their work to heart, to search their souls, to pray, and to touch the mystery.

If they have the courage to accept this invitation, eventually they begin to experience personally what they may have been telling others about for half a lifetime: the messianic empowerment which comes with Passingover. They also experience personally what the prophets were talking about when they spoke out against an extraverted and self-confident approach to religion. As these chastened women and men come from the place of "letting-be" to tell us the dreams they dream, the visions they see, and the mystery which animates their lives; and to serve us once again in love, they are like women and men coming up out of the desert. We would do well to watch and pray for their coming, for the spiritual renewal of our religious communities today depends on the mystery which these chastened persons bring, once again, to ministry. By the messianic quality of their lives, these "wounded healers" are living reminders to us that the power of the New Creation comes through the experience of our own human weakness. By personifying the Art of Passingover in this way, these "Christophers"—"Messiah-bearers"—are also living invitations to us to do the same ourselves.

Growing Toward a New Creation

Not all of us who go into the desert of "letting-be" are ministers or artists, but all of us who come out of it are; we are artists in the Art of Passingover. We are learning how to live and act more gracefully and creatively in this world by continually "letting-go" in trust, "letting-be" in hope, and "letting grow" in love. As we become more proficient in this Art, our life and the life of the world around us begin to be messianically transformed into a completely New Creation.

Prior to going into the desert, some of us may have been so arrogant as to claim that we not only knew of, but also belonged to, the country, the race, or the religion which had exclusive rights on hosting the New Creation. Others of us, if we thought of it at all, may have thought that the New Creation was taking place somewhere else, and had nothing to do with the world in which we live. In our more imaginative moments we may have imagined it taking place in church, but in our most wildly imaginative moments we never conceived of it taking place in our own lives, much less in the marketplace. As we come up out of the desert in communion and creative commitment, however, we know better. We know that the New Creation takes place wherever, and whenever, persons have the messianic courage to "let go" in trust, to "let be" in hope, and to "let grow" in love. To that, we continue to say *"Amen"* and *"Alleluia"* with our lives.

Conclusion

The Creed Becomes a Gloria

I am no longer trying for perfection
by my own efforts. . . .
All I want is to know Christ
and the power of his resurrection
and to share his sufferings
by reproducing the pattern of his death.
That is the way I can hope
to take my place
in the resurrection of the dead.
Philippians 3:9–11
(Jerusalem Bible)

We began our reflection on the Art of Passingover with this text from Paul, and with a "little creed" which might carry much more meaning for us now, than it did at first:

I believe that everyone is called to live creatively;
I believe that living creatively requires that we practice
    the Art of Passingover;
I believe that the Art of Passingover involves:
    "Letting-go" in trust,
    "Letting-be" in hope,
    "Letting-grow" in love;
I believe that, in practicing the Art of Passingover,
    we are animated by, and commune with, Life Itself;
I believe that, by practicing the Art of Passingover,
    our lives are renewed, our world is re-created,
    and the Messiah comes.

As we practice the Art of Passingover, our life begins saying "*Amen*" to this little creed.

197

In time, our creed starts becoming a *Gloria*, as what is sown in tears is reaped in joy; as what dies within us comes to life again; as what goes inward in suffering comes outward in service; as what goes down in pain comes up in praise. Then we find our life beginning to say *"Alleluia"* through the Art of Passingover:

> In "letting-go" . . . praise . . .
> In "letting-be" . . . praise . . .
> In "letting-grow" . . . praise . . .

Since the Art of Passingover continues to go on until all of creation is just one glorious *"Alleluia,"* this *"Alleluia"* of ours is not really a conclusion; it is merely a foretaste of what is to come.

> Glory be to him
> whose power,
> working in us
> can do infinitely more
> than we can ask
> or imagine. . . .
>   *Ephesians 3:20*
>   *(New American Bible)*

Appendix

Meditative Exercises in the Art of Passingover

Each of the following exercises can help us internalize the Art of Passingover by letting us meditatively explore one of its basic experiences in our own life. Before beginning each exercise, it is good to take a comfortable position and to take some time to become quiet. It is also good to take brief notes either during or immediately after each meditation, and to read them back afterward, adding whatever else comes to mind. The questions below are not "head questions" which ask for a clear answer; they are "heart questions" which invite you to explore your own experience at many different levels.

Exercise 1
The Art of Passingover

Channel One: Personal Experience

Become quiet and list several personal experiences of Passingover. In a meditative way, re-enter one of these experiences and describe more fully what it was like and how it felt.

Channel Two: Messianic Experience

Does your personal experience of Passingover lead you to experience something on Channel Two: a passage of Scripture, or an event, or a person with more-than-personal significance in your life? If so, read the passage or describe the event or the person, noting whatever else comes to you as you do so.

The Stereo Effect

What comes to you as you listen to both channels of experience at the same time?

The Stereo Response

How do you respond to what you have experienced on both channels?

Review

Read what you have written, adding to it anything else that comes to mind.

Exercise 2
"Letting-Go": The Experience of Painful Endings

Channel One: Personal Experience

Become quiet and list several personal experiences of "letting-go." They need not have been voluntary. As a spiritual pilgrim, re-enter one of these experiences and describe more fully what it was like and how it felt.

Channel Two: Messianic Experience

Meditatively read one of the following Scripture passages, noting what you hear, think, feel, and experience in an inner way:
    Genesis 12:1–4
    Isaiah 52:13–53:12
    Psalm 22:1–22
    Psalm 69:1–22
    Lamentations 3
    1 Corinthians 1:10–25
    Mark 15:1–5
    Matthew 26:36–56

The Stereo Effect

What comes to you as you listen meditatively to the experience of "letting-go" on both channels at the same time?

The Stereo Response

How do you respond to what you hear on both channels? Is your life currently inviting you to "let go" in trust in some way? If so, how do you respond?

Review

Review what you have written, adding to it anything else that comes to mind.

Exercise 3
"Letting-Be": The Experience of Awkward Inbetweens

Channel 1: Personal Experience

Become quiet and list several personal experiences of "letting-be." As a spiritual pilgrim, re-enter one of these experiences and describe more fully what it was like and how it felt.

Channel 2: The Messianic Experience

Meditatively read one of the following passages, noting what you hear, think, feel, and experience in an inner way:

    Exodus 16:1–3
    Exodus 33:7–23
    Psalm 13
    Psalm 130
    Psalm 131
    Ezekiel 37:1–3
    Acts 9:1–9
    Mark 9:2–10
    Luke 1:16–22
    Luke 2:19
    Luke 4:1–13

The Stereo Effect

What comes to you as you listen meditatively to both channels at the same time?

The Stereo Response

How do you respond to what you hear on both channels? Is your life currently inviting you to "let be" in hope in some way? If so, how do you respond?

Review

Review what you have written and add to it anything else that comes to mind.

Exercise 4
"Letting-Grow": The Experience of Awesome Beginnings and Unfoldings

Channel 1: Personal Experience

Become quiet and list several personal experiences of "letting-grow." As a spiritual pilgrim, re-enter one of these experiences and describe in more detail what it was like, how it unfolded, and how it made you feel.

Channel 2: The Messianic Experience

Meditatively read one of the following passages, noting what you hear, think, feel, and experience in an inner way:

Exodus 34:27–35
Ezekiel 37:5–14
Jeremiah 31:1–14
Jeremiah 31:31–34
Isaiah 11
Isaiah 40:1–11
Isaiah 42:1–9
Isaiah 43:1–8
Isaiah 48:1–11
Isaiah 54
Psalm 22:23–32
Psalm 69:30–37

Psalm 135
Psalm 136
Psalm 138
Psalm 148
Psalm 150
Romans 6:3–11
Acts 2:1–8
Acts 3:1–10
Acts 10
Luke 1:46–55
John 20:19–29
John 21:15–19
Revelation 21:1–7

The Stereo Effect

What comes to you as you listen meditatively to both channels at the same time?

The Stereo Response

How do you respond to what you hear on both channels? Is your life currently inviting you to "let grow" in love in some way? If so, how do you respond?

Review

Review what you have written, adding to it anything else that comes to mind.

Exercise 5
Personifying the Art of Passingover

Channel 1: Personal Experience

Become quiet and describe where you are now in responding to the invitation to live creatively.

Channel 2: The Messianic Experience

Does your present experience lead you to experience something on Channel Two: a passage of Scripture, or an event, or a person of more-than-personal significance in your life? If so, meditatively read the passage or describe the event or person, noting whatever comes to you as you do so.

The Stereo Effect

What comes to you as you listen meditatively to both channels at the same time?

The Stereo Response

How do you respond to what you hear on both channels?

Review

Review what you have written, adding to it anything else that comes to mind.